The Nuremberg Trials

Other books in the At Issue in History series:

The Nuremberg Trials

Mitchell Bard, *Book Editor*

Daniel Leone, *President*
Bonnie Szumski, *Publisher*
Scott Barbour, *Managing Editor*

OPPOSING VIEWPOINTS® SERIES

AT ISSUE IN HISTORY

Greenhaven Press, Inc.
San Diego, California

WITHDRAWN

Library of Congress Cataloging-in-Publication Data

The Nuremberg trials / Mitchell Bard, book editor.
      p.   cm. — (At issue in history)
    Includes bibliographical references and index.
    ISBN 0-7377-1057-8 (pbk. : alk. paper) —
ISBN 0-7377-1058-6 (lib. : alk. paper)
    1. Nuremberg Trial of Major German War Criminals, Nuremberg, Germany, 1945–1946. 2. War crime trials—Germany—Nuremberg—History. I. Bard, Mitchell, 1959–
II. Series.

KZ1176 .N87 2002
341.6'9'0268—dc21

                                    2001033509

© 2002 by Greenhaven Press, Inc.
10911 Technology Place, San Diego, CA 92127

Printed in the U.S.A.

Contents

Foreword

Historian Robert Weiss defines history simply as "a record and interpretation of past events." Both elements—record and interpretation—are necessary, Weiss argues.

> Names, dates, places, and events are the essence of history. But historical writing is not a compendium of facts. It consists of facts placed in a sequence to tell a connected story. A work of history is not merely a story, however. It also must analyze what happened and *why*—that is, it must interpret the past for the reader.

For example, the events of December 7, 1941, that led President Franklin D. Roosevelt to call it "a date which will live in infamy" are fairly well known and straightforward. A force of Japanese planes and submarines launched a torpedo and bombing attack on American military targets in Pearl Harbor, Hawaii. The surprise assault sank five battleships, disabled or sank fourteen additional ships, and left almost twenty-four hundred American soldiers and sailors dead. On the following day, the United States formally entered World War II when Congress declared war on Japan.

These facts and consequences were almost immediately communicated to the American people who heard reports about Pearl Harbor and President Roosevelt's response on the radio. All realized that this was an important and pivotal event in American and world history. Yet the news from Pearl Harbor raised many unanswered questions. Why did Japan decide to launch such an offensive? Why were the attackers so successful in catching America by surprise? What did the attack reveal about the two nations, their people, and their leadership? What were its causes, and what were its effects? Political leaders, academic historians, and students look to learn the basic facts of historical events and to read the intepretations of these events by many different sources, both primary and secondary, in order to develop a more complete picture of the event in a historical context.

In the case of Pearl Harbor, several important questions surrounding the event remain in dispute, most notably the role of President Roosevelt. Some historians have blamed his policies for deliberately provoking Japan to attack in order to propel America into World War II; a few have gone so far as to accuse him of knowing of the impending attack but not informing others. Other historians, examining the same event, have exonerated the president of such charges, arguing that the historical evidence does not support such a theory.

The Greenhaven At Issue in History series recognizes that many important historical events have been interpreted differently and in some cases remain shrouded in controversy. Each volume features a collection of articles that focus on a topic that has sparked controversy among eyewitnesses, contemporary observers, and historians. An introductory essay sets the stage for each topic by presenting background and context. Several chapters then examine different facets of the subject at hand with readings chosen for their diversity of opinion. Each selection is preceded by a summary of the author's main points and conclusions. A bibliography is included for those students interested in pursuing further research. An annotated table of contents and thorough index help readers to quickly locate material of interest. Taken together, the contents of each of the volumes in the Greenhaven At Issue in History series will help students become more discriminating and thoughtful readers of history.

Introduction

During World War II, the U.S. government decided not to pursue German war criminals until after an Allied victory for fear of provoking reprisals against prisoners of war. Instead, officials secretly gathered evidence of war crimes for use after the war. At times the United States issued threats that it would punish the Germans for their actions, but the failure to do anything—such as capture and try Nazi officials or prisoners of war—led Hitler and his minions to believe the West would do nothing and that they could mistreat their prisoners, civilians, and combatants with impunity.

Once the war was won, the Allies were prepared to carry out their threats. The fact that Germany had waged a war that had cost millions of lives and hundreds of billions of dollars in damages was sufficient reason to hold officials accountable. The liberation of the concentration camps and revelations about the extent of the horrors of the Holocaust added an additional moral imperative to proceeding against the perpetrators. As President Dwight D. Eisenhower said in a press conference on June 18, 1945:

> When I found the first camp like that I think I was never so angry in my life. The bestiality displayed there was not merely piled up bodies of people that had starved to death, but to follow out the road, and see where they tried to evacuate them so they could still work, you could see where they were sprawled on the road. You could go to their burial pits and see horrors that really I wouldn't even want to begin to describe. I think people ought to know about such things. It explains something of my attitude toward the German war criminal. I believe he must be punished, and I will hold out for that forever.

Many Allied officials, including Winston Churchill and Josef Stalin, would have been happy to summarily execute Germans captured after the war. The four major powers—

Great Britain, France, the Soviet Union, and the United States—decided to put them on trial instead.

The United Nations formed a War Crimes Commission in October 1943 to begin gathering evidence for postwar trials and to develop a list of war criminals. When the war ended, representatives of the four governments met and negotiated the ground rules for a trial of what they considered the "major" war criminals. The negotiations were influenced nearly as much by political considerations as legal ones, but an agreement was struck whereby an International Military Tribunal would be created to prosecute Nazis for the common plan or conspiracy to wage aggressive war in violation of international law or treaties; planning, preparation, or waging an aggressive war; violations of the international rules of war; and crimes against humanity.

The Allies' motivation for holding a trial was to set an example for the future, to show that crimes of the magnitude committed during the war would not go unpunished. They wanted to show they could resist the temptation to exact vengeance and instead uphold the rule of law. They also sought to hold the superior officers accountable for the actions of their underlings. Furthermore, they desired to make clear that such serious crimes could not be excused by the claim that a person was "just following orders."

Whom to Try?

One of the most difficult decisions involved who should be tried. Most Nazis who might have been tried for war crimes either evaded capture, were purposely allowed to flee to the United States and other countries, or were simply not pursued.

The most wanted man, of course, was Hitler himself, but he committed suicide. So did Hitler's preferred successor, Joseph Goebbels, and Heinrich Himmler, the head of the Gestapo and SS. Hitler's second in command, Martin Bormann, was ordered to flee and never was captured. He was believed to have died in 1945. Adolf Eichmann, one of the principal architects of the Final Solution, escaped to Argentina, where he lived peacefully until being kidnapped by Israeli agents in 1960 and brought to Jerusalem, where he was tried, convicted, and executed for war crimes.

In the end, twenty-two men were chosen to represent the top echelon of the Reich. Their trial was conducted at

Nuremberg between October 20, 1945, and October 1, 1946. Many officials were missing, such as Rudolf Hess, the commandant of Auschwitz. Among the defendants at Nuremberg were eight jurists, one university professor, and one dentist. All of them were very well educated. In addition to the aforementioned Bormann, who was tried in absentia, the other defendants were:

- Karl Dönitz—Supreme Commander of the Navy; in Hitler's last will and testament he was made president of the Third Reich and supreme commander of the Armed Forces.
- Hans Frank—Governor-general of occupied Poland.
- Wilhelm Frick—Minister of the Interior.
- Hans Fritzsche—Ministerial director and head of the radio division in the Propaganda Ministry.
- Walther Funk—President of the Reichsbank.
- Hermann Goering—Reichsmarschall, chief of the Air Force.
- Rudolf Hess—Deputy to Hitler.
- Alfred Jodl—Chief of Army Operations.
- Ernst Kaltenbrunner—Chief of Reich Main Security Office, whose departments included the Gestapo and SS.
- Wilhelm Keitel—Chief of staff of the high command of the Armed Forces.
- Erich Raeder—Grand admiral of the Navy.
- Alfred Rosenberg—Minister of the occupied eastern territories.
- Fritz Sauckel—Labor leader.
- Hjalmar Schacht—Minister of economics.
- Arthur Seyss-Inquart—Commisar of the Netherlands.
- Albert Speer—Minister of Armaments and War Production.
- Julius Streicher—Editor of the newspaper *Der Stürmer*, director of the Central Committee for the Defense against Jewish Atrocity and Boycott Propaganda.
- Constantin von Neurath—Protector of Bohemia and Moravia.
- Franz von Papen—One-time chancellor of Germany.
- Joachim von Ribbentrop—Minister of foreign affairs.
- Baldur von Schirach—Reich Youth leader.

While today Holocaust deniers claim the atrocities of the war did not happen or try to minimize them, the defendants did no such thing. They did not refute the evidence. Some did say they had no knowledge of some events or complained they were singled out for committing the same acts as others who escaped arrest. Others hid behind the argument that they were only following orders and were therefore not responsible for their actions or those of their subordinates.

Ensuring a Fair Trial

The Allies (particularly the United States) were determined to make the trial a fair one rather than just a show trial as a prelude to the victors' exacting vengeance on the vanquished. Therefore, though the actions of the Nazis were well-known, the prosecution sought to develop sufficient evidence to leave no doubt as to the guilt of the individual defendants. Since the war had only recently ended, this was a more difficult task than one might expect. The prosecution had to collect, collate, and analyze tens of thousands of documents and the testimony of witnesses. The Germans had helped by keeping impeccable records of virtually everything they did. On the other hand, the documents rarely specified the name of particular killers. In addition, as their eventual defeat had become inevitable, the Nazis had done everything possible to destroy the evidence of their crimes and an unknown number of documents had literally gone up in smoke.

One measure taken to ensure fairness was to conduct the trial in the open. The press, the German people, and the general public were all able to witness every part of the trial. The transcripts and documents were also available, so no one could accuse the Allies of misconduct.

Just as it has been said that democracy is the worst form of government except for all the other types, the Nuremberg Trial was an imperfect tribunal, but still more just by legal standards than perhaps any other created to adjudicate war crimes. And, in the end, the Nazis received the kind of trial they denied to those they prosecuted and persecuted.

The fairness of the trial was evident in the fact that three of the defendants were acquitted. Still, the evidence was so overwhelming that eleven were given the death penalty, three were sentenced to life imprisonment, and four received prison terms ranging from ten to twenty years. Those sentenced to death were hanged (except Goering, who committed suicide in his cell) at Spandau Prison on October 6, 1946. Those acquitted were placed in a denazification program following the trial. Those who received prison sentences were sent to Spandau Prison.

These sentences were carried out with only a few exceptions. The exceptions were von Neurath, who was sentenced to fifteen years but became ill and was released in 1954 (he died in 1956); Raeder, who served less than ten years of his life sentence (and died in 1960); and Funk, who was also in failing health and was paroled in 1957 (and also died in 1960). After 1966, the sole inmate of Spandau Prison was Hess, who committed suicide in 1987 at the age of ninety-two. The other convicted men were either executed or served their full sentences.

Other Trials

When people speak of *the* Nuremberg Trial, they usually refer to the trial of the 22 high-ranking Nazis. In fact, 12 other major trials were conducted at Nuremberg involving 185 defendants, including some of the German industrialists who aided the war effort, the *Einsatzgruppen* (the mobile killing squads), concentration camp administrators and the doctors responsible for gruesome medical experiments. A number of other trials were held elsewhere. These included trials of officials from POW and concentration camps and lower-ranking officials.

Although most of the verdicts stood after the original Nuremberg Trial, in many of the subsequent cases Nazis found guilty of war crimes did not suffer the punishments imposed at trial. John J. McCloy, the U.S. High Commissioner for Germany, was pressured by the Pope, the German government, and others to grant clemency to some of the criminals. He subsequently commuted or reduced the sentences of all convicted concentration camp doctors, twenty of the twenty-five SS officers convicted of serving in the *Einsatzgruppen*, industrialist Alfred Krupp, and Ernst von Weizsacker, a Nazi foreign office official convicted of complicity in the deaths of six thousand Jews. Michael Berenbaum, the former project director of the United States Holocaust Memorial Museum, explained:

> While the trials were in progress public attention shifted to the unfolding of the Cold War, the struggle between the United States and the Soviet Union that seemed to embody a worldwide battle between capi-

talism and Marxism. The 1948 Berlin Blockade made the future of Germany central to American geopolitical interests. The American government did not want to provoke the German people, especially when their support was vital to the future. The Korean War only intensified the desire to get on to other things. Interest in the trials faded. No sooner had they ended than clemency boards were established. In the next few years, sentences were reduced, pardons were granted and time off was given for good behavior.

A Precedent Is Set

One precedent set by Nuremberg was that there should be no statute of limitations on war crimes; consequently, some war criminals are still being pursued and tried. In recent years, several high profile trials have been conducted. For example, Klaus Barbie ("the Butcher of Lyons") was involved in deporting thousands of French Jews to extermination camps in Poland and murdering members of the French Resistance movement. In 1983 he was extradited from Bolivia to France for prosecution. He was convicted and sentenced to life imprisonment.

As many as ten thousand Nazi war criminals are believed to have fled to the United States. Some entered the country under false pretenses, hiding their past. Others were welcomed because of their presumed value in fighting the Soviet Union or were given protection because of alleged or anticipated Soviet persecution. The U.S. government facilitated the entry of many Nazis and hired them as scientists to work on top-secret projects—despite their past involvement in war crimes—because their expertise was needed.

Though the United States cannot try former Nazis for their crimes, an Office of Special Investigations (OSI) was set up to investigate those who went to America illegally, using either false documents or lying on their immigration forms. If OSI proves their guilt, they may be deported to their countries of origin, which may try them for their war activities. One question that is sometimes asked is why OSI pursues old men who have lived peaceful, lawful lives in America. The former OSI director explains that going after these men is justified because their crimes cannot be forgiven or forgotten: "The fact that an individual got away so long didn't diminish or mitigate his crimes," Neal Sher said in an interview with the editor. "If, forty years from now, the perpetrator of some horrible crime was found, no one would say 'don't prosecute.'"

Nuremberg's Legacy

The larger objective of all the trials was to deter future wars and wartime atrocities. In 1948, the United Nations adopted the Convention for the Prevention of Crimes of Genocide. This international code was a response to the Nuremberg defendants' claims that their actions had not violated any laws. The convention specifically defined many of the types of actions taken by the Nazis as crimes, such as killing people from a particular group, forcibly removing or transferring children from a group, or taking measures that would lead to the extermination of a particular group. Ironically, the United States, one of the champions of these ideals, and one of the prosecutors of the Nuremberg Trial, was one of the last nations to ratify the convention. It was more than forty years later, in November 1988, when President Ronald Reagan made the United States the eighty-ninth nation to ratify the treaty.

The Genocide Convention has had little impact on international behavior, and the record since Nuremberg indicates that the Allies failed to accomplish their lofty vision. In fact, they were among the perpetrators of subsequent abuses. The Soviet Union committed war crimes throughout its reign of terror, and while their actions are in no way comparable to those of the Soviets, the Western nations earned more than a few blemishes on their record during their involvement in places like Ireland, Palestine, and Vietnam. Though nothing may compare to the Holocaust, that was not the last instance of genocide in the twentieth century. Nuremberg did nothing to prevent ethnic cleansing in the Balkans, tribal massacres in Rwanda, or mass murder in Cambodia. Still, the principles of Nuremberg are being used as the foundation for new tribunals aimed at punishing the war crimes of today, and with the same noble ambition of putting an end to wars so that there can be no war crimes.

Chapter 1

The Decision to Try the Nazis

1

Bringing Nazis to Justice

Robert E. Conot

Although the Allies could be criticized for not doing more to save the Jews during the war, they did not ignore the Germans' actions. Beginning at the end of 1942, Roosevelt and Churchill expressed their horror at the behavior of the Nazis and vowed to bring the Nazi criminals to justice. However, these statements seemed like little more than idle threats since no action was being taken. The idea to gather evidence and put the Nazis on trial evolved slowly. The United States led the effort to conduct a hearing, in part to serve as a means of documenting the atrocities for posterity. The British, at least initially, favored summarily executing the men responsible for the war and genocide. This excerpt by Robert E. Conot traces the development of the concept of holding a war crimes trial in Nuremberg and the process involved in choosing the defendants. Conot is the author of *Justice at Nuremberg*, from which this selection was taken.

Nearly two years had passed since President Roosevelt, on October 7, 1942, had first declared: "It is our intention that just and sure punishment shall be meted out to the ringleaders responsible for the organized murder of thousands of innocent persons in the commission of atrocities which have violated every tenet of the Christian faith." Two months later, on December 17, British Foreign Secretary Anthony Eden had told the House of Commons: "The German authorities are now carrying into effect Hitler's oft repeated intention to exterminate the Jewish people of Europe. From all the occupied centers of Europe Jews are being transported in conditions of appalling horror and brutality to eastern Europe. In Poland, which has been made the principal Nazi slaughterhouse, the ghettos established by the Nazi invaders are being systematically emptied of all Jews except a few highly skilled workers required for war industries. None of those taken away are ever heard of again. The ablebodied are slowly worked to death in labor camps. The infirm are left to die of exposure and starvation, or are deliberately massacred in mass executions."

The next year, Roosevelt, Churchill, and Stalin formally stated in the Moscow Declaration their determination to bring the guilty to justice. On October 26, 1943, the United Nations War Crimes Commission, composed of fifteen Allied nations (not including the Soviet Union) held its first meeting in London. Again, on March 24, 1944, Roosevelt warned: "None who participate in these acts of savagery shall go unpunished. All who share in the guilt shall share the punishment."

Yet nothing had been done to implement the multitude of declarations. Morgenthau was bitter at the State Department for its bureaucratic bumbling and failure to facilitate the escape of Jews; and President Roosevelt was concerned about the possible loss of the Jewish vote in an election year. In the weeks following the Normandy landing on June 6, Eisenhower became more and more incensed as scores of British, Canadian, and American prisoners of war were shot by the Waffen SS in what seemed like calculated policy. In Washington, G-1, the Office of the Chief of Staff of the Personnel Division, was charged with collecting evidence on crimes committed against American servicemen. In July, the task was delegated to Lieutenant Colonel Murray C. Bernays; and Bernays was to prove the guiding spirit leading the way to the Nuremberg trial. . . .

Execution vs. Trial

On July 11, Churchill had written to Foreign Secretary Anthony Eden: "There is no doubt that this is probably the greatest and most horrible crime ever committed in the whole history of the world, and it has been done by scientific machinery by nominally civilized men in the name of a great State. . . . It is quite clear that all concerned who may fall into our hands, including the people who only obeyed orders by carrying out the butcheries, should be put to death after their association with the murders has been proved."

Morgenthau, who advocated the division and deindustrialization of Germany, concurred with Churchill and the British Lord Chancellor, John Simon, that the principal Nazi leaders should be charged with their crimes, then summarily shot. On the other hand, Colonel Mickey Marcus of the Army Civil Affairs Division, which was charged with formulating postwar policy for Germany, was disturbed by Morgenthau's emotional approach. At a meeting with Bernays, he agreed that retribution must not appear to be a Judaic act of revenge. Summary execution, no matter how justified, could never serve as a substitute for justice.

Bernays proposed that an international tribunal should be established to condemn violence, terror, racism, totalitarianism, and wanton destruction.

"Not to try these beasts would be to miss the educational and therapeutic opportunity of our generation," Bernays argued. "They must be tried not alone for their specific aims, but for the bestiality from which these crimes sprang.". . .

Bernays proposed that an international tribunal should be established to condemn violence, terror, racism, totalitarianism, and wanton destruction; the tribunal should arouse the German people to a sense of their guilt and a realization of their responsibility. Otherwise, Germany would simply have lost another war; the German people would not come to understand the barbarism they had supported, nor have any conception of the criminal character of the Nazi regime. The fascist potential would remain undiminished, and the menace remain. Only the staging of a great trial—or, possibly, a number of trials—in which the conspiracy of the Nazi leadership would be proved and the utilization of the Nazi organizations in the furtherance of that conspiracy would be established, could all the objectives be attained, and all criminals, large and small, be caught in the same web. . . .

Churchill and Lord Simon stuck to the proposition that "it is beyond question that Hitler and a number of arch criminals associated with him [including Mussolini, Himmler, Goering, Ribbentrop, and Goebbels] must, so far as they fall into Allied hands, suffer the penalty of death for their conduct leading up to the war and for their wickedness in the conduct of the war. It being conceded that these leaders must suffer death, the question arises whether they should be tried by some form of tribunal claiming to exercise judicial functions, or whether the decision taken by the Allies should be reached and enforced without the machinery of a trial."

After weighing the pros and cons, the British concluded once more that the dangers of a trial outweighed the advantages and that "execution without trial is the preferable course.". . .

On April 30, 1945, however, Hitler had committed suicide and been followed by Goebbels. Mussolini was captured and executed by Italian partisans. Two weeks later Himmler bit into a capsule of cyanide. With these men dead, the British opposition to a trial softened. . . .

Deciding Where and How to Try the Nazis

The British suggested that the trial might be held in Munich, the cradle of the Nazi movement; or, alternately, in Berlin or Leipzig. Jackson replied that he had no objection to Munich, which was in the American zone, but that the United States did not want the trial held in either of the other two cities, which were under Russian occupation. David Maxwell-Fyfe proposed ten top Nazis as defendants: Hermann Goering, commander of the Luftwaffe, director of the Four Year Plan, founder of the Gestapo, and onetime heir apparent to Adolf Hitler; Rudolf Hess, party secretary and Hitler's right-hand man until 1941, when he had mysteriously parachuted from a Messerschmitt fighter over Scotland; Joachim von Ribbentrop, the foreign minister; Robert Ley, director of the German Labor Front; Alfred Rosenberg, party theoretician and minister for the Occupied Eastern Territories; Wilhelm Frick, interior minister; Field Marshal Wilhelm Keitel, chief of staff of the Wehrmacht; Julius Streicher, a gauleiter and notorious Jew baiter; Ernst Kaltenbrunner, head of the Reich Security Office, the second-ranking man in the SS after Himmler; and Hans Frank, governor of occupied Poland. . . .

The Anglo-American system of trial had little in common with the continental, followed by the French and Russians. Jackson was as ill-informed about continental practices as Major General I.T. Nikitchenko, the forty-five-year-old head of the Soviet delegation, was about American; and repeatedly one was unable to comprehend the other. Furthermore, it quickly became clear that the American and Soviet conceptions of the International Military Tribunal were startlingly at odds.

The Anglo-American system of trial had little in common with the continental.

Nikitchenko maintained: "We are dealing here with the chief war criminals who have already been convicted by both the Moscow and Crimea [Yalta] declarations." The job of the court was merely to decide the degree of guilt of each individual, and to mete out punishment. The essence of the case would be determined before the start of the trial—in the continental system, the prosecutor assembled all evidence both against and in favor of the accused and presented it to an examining judge, who then decided whether the person should be brought to trial. If the judge ruled in the affirmative, he was, in effect, finding the person guilty, so that the burden of proof from then on rested on the defendant.

Unlike procedure in Anglo-American law, where the prosecutor and defense counsel are adversaries, with the judge acting as arbiter, in continental law prosecutor, defense counsel, and judge are all charged with the task of arriving at the truth. . . .

Nikitchenko's conception of the trial so shocked Jackson that he suggested, on June 29, that the best thing might be for each nation to go ahead and try the Nazis it held in custody according to its own customs.

The following day he recovered sufficiently to reiterate the American position that it was "necessary to authenticate by methods of the highest accuracy the whole history of the Nazi movement, its extermination of minorities, its aggression against neighbors, its treachery and its barbarism. . . . We envision it as a trial of the master planners.". . .

The next day produced new disagreement. SHAEF (Supreme Headquarters Allied Expeditionary Force) had conducted a survey of German cities as possible sites for the trial, Jackson revealed. The only undamaged facilities extensive enough to accommodate the trial were in Nuremberg, so Nuremberg should be selected as the location. . . .

The Nazi leadership was indicted for (1) Crimes Against Peace, including the launching of an aggressive war; (2) War Crimes, that is, acts contrary to acceptable usages and against the provisions of the Hague and Geneva conventions; and (3) Crimes Against Humanity, covering any and all atrocities committed by the regime during its reign. . . .

The most spectacular of the finds were the records of Alfred Rosenberg, providing a detailed description of German operations in the East and of the looting of the various occupied territories. Discovered hidden beneath wet straw behind a wall in a Bavarian barn by an OSS lieutenant seeking photographic material, the forty-seven crates were flown to Paris, where Jackson had set up his continental document-collecting center. Though, by the end of July, the contents of the crates had been only cursorily examined, one of Bernays's investigators wrote him: "This is an almost unbelievable admission of *systematic* killings, looting, etc.". . .

The Accused

Bernays had compiled a master list of the major German war criminals; the number stood at 122. On the first ten of these, Goering, Hess, Ribbentrop, Ley, Rosenberg, Frick, Keitel, Streicher, Kaltenbrunner, and Frank, suggested originally by the British, the Americans immediately agreed. Only Hess, because of his disoriented mental condition, posed a question mark. The Americans proposed five others: Admiral Karl Doenitz, head of the submarine service until his elevation to command of the entire Nazi navy in January 1943; Arthur Seyss-Inquart, an Austrian who had played a pivotal role in Hitler's Anschluss in 1938 and subsequently had been head of the German administration in the occupied Netherlands; Albert Speer, chief of Nazi war production during the last three and one-half years of the war; Hjalmar Schacht, economics minister and head of the Reichsbank during the first five years of the Hitler regime; and Walther Funk, who had replaced Schacht as minister of economics and president of the Reichsbank. The latter three primarily interested the Americans, with their emphasis on the economic aspects of the Nazi aggression; but the British had no objection to them.

Almost everyone on the American and British delegations had his favorite candidate, and lists were compiled periodically. But by August 8, when the charter was signed, only Martin Bormann, who had succeeded Hess as party secretary, had been added. Since all the men were to be charged with a conspiracy, it was thought proper, and perhaps necessary, to list Hitler at the head of the group. The prosecutorial staff, nevertheless, hesitated to include him, for—although there was little doubt that he had killed himself—they feared that to do so might generate rumors of his survival.

No criteria had been established for inclusion in the list of defendants, and additions were arbitrary. The British suggested Baldur von Schirach, organizer and leader of the Hitler Youth, and subsequently gauleiter of Vienna. The Americans, adhering to the concept that each of the individual organizations should be represented by one or more of its leaders, had named Keitel for the armed forces, Doenitz the navy, and Goering the Luftwaffe, but were missing a man for the army. So General Alfred Jodl, the chief of the Wehrmacht operations staff, was included.

The OSS thought that to present a true panorama of Nazi crimes at least thirty defendants, including several industrialists, would have to be selected. The best known was Alfried Krupp, operating head of the world-famous armaments firm. His name was added, as was that of Fritz Sauckel, who had impressed workers from all over Europe into Hitler's labor program. By mid-August, however, no final determination had been made, and Jackson's list of potential defendants still contained seventy-three names.

After thinking the matter over, Jackson decided there was no point in trying a dead man, and dropped Hitler. However, Franz von Papen, who had preceded Hitler as chancellor and briefly been vice-chancellor in Hitler's cabinet, was tacked on.

When the tentative list was shown to the French and Russians in the third week of August, the French were chagrined that it contained no German held by them, and combed their roster for a candidate. They came up with Baron Constantin von Neurath, who had been living in retirement upon his estate in Württemberg, which was part of the French occupation zone. Neurath's tenure as Protector of Bohemia and Moravia and head of a "Secret Cabinet

Council" placed him under suspicion. No one on the Allied staffs knew what this cabinet council had consisted of; but it sounded appropriately menacing.

On August 25, Jackson, Fyfe, Gros, and Nikitchenko agreed on a list of twenty-two defendants. Twenty-one were in custody. The twenty-second, Bormann, had, according to rumors, been captured by the Russians. Jackson repeatedly questioned Nikitchenko whether the Russians held Bormann; but Nikitchenko did not know, and apparently could not find out. A press release naming the accused was prepared, and about to be released on August 28, when Nikitchenko rushed in to announce that the Soviets did not hold Bormann, but that they had captured two Germans whom they wanted added to the list.

First was Admiral Erich Raeder, commander of the German navy until January 1943. Raeder had been a marginal candidate for the trial, so far as the British and Americans were concerned, but had gained importance by the discovery of a document indicating he had been a prime instigator of the invasion of Norway.

The other was Hans Fritzsche, a popular newscaster and second-rank official in Goebbels' Propaganda Ministry, who had not been on any of the many lists of top war criminals. Had he been suggested by a member of the American or British prosecutorial staffs, he would have been summarily rejected. But since the Americans were contributing thirteen defendants, the British seven, and the French one, it was a matter of national pride to the Russians that they be permitted at least two.

In the interim, the Americans had second thoughts about naming thirty-eight-year-old Alfried Krupp, who had been active in the company's affairs only since the start of the war, rather than his seventy-five-year-old father, Baron Gustav Krupp von Bohlen und Halbach. At the last moment, Gustav's name was substituted for Alfried's. It turned out to be an incredible error, but one typical of a case in which the charges were prepared and the defendants chosen before the facts had been more than cursorily investigated.

On August 30, the list of Nazi leaders selected for the first trial was released to the press.

2

The Creation of the Tribunal and the Law Behind It

Court TV

The Nuremberg Trial combined elements of Anglo-American and continental law, which differ significantly. This brief article by Court TV describes the background behind the creation of the tribunal and lays out some of the differences between the Nuremberg Trial and a typical American trial.

During World War II, the Allies and representatives of the exiled governments of occupied Europe met several times to discuss post-war treatment of the Nazi leaders. Initially, most of the Allies considered their crimes to have been beyond the scope of human justice—that their fate was a political, rather than a legal, question.

Winston Churchill, for example, said in 1944 that they should be "hunted down and shot." The French and Soviets also supported summary executions. The Americans, however, pushed for a trial. (A faction within the U.S. government led by Secretary of War Henry L. Stimson had won a domestic battle over the U.S. position on punishment of the Nazis. The other faction, led by Henry Morgenthau, the Jewish secretary of the Treasury, supported a harsh plan designed to prevent Germany from ever rising again as an industrial power.)

In August 1945, the British, French, Americans and Soviets, meeting in London, signed the agreement that cre-

From "The Creation of the Tribunal and the Law Behind It," an article on the Court TV website: www.courttv.com/casefiles/nuremberg/law.html. Copyright © 1999 Courtroom Television Network LLC. Reprinted with permission.

ated the Nuremberg court, officially the International Military Tribunal, and set ground rules for the trial. The London Charter of the International Military Tribunal was named to avoid using words such as "law" or "code" in an effort to circumvent the delicate question of whether the trial would be ex post facto [retroactive].

The London Charter set down the rules of trial procedure and defined the crimes to be tried. (It did not define the term "criminal organizations," although six organizations were indicted under the charter.)

The defendants were charged not only for the systematic butchering of millions of people, but also for planning and carrying out the war in Europe.

The Law

The International Military Tribunal combined elements of Anglo-American and civil (continental) law. Defendants' rights and the rules of evidence differed in several ways from those in American courtrooms:

- In contrast to the U.S. system, in which the prosecutors must show evidence suggesting there is probable cause to try a defendant, civil law requires that all proof be presented with the indictment. At the International Military Tribunal, some of the proof was presented at the time of indictment, some was not.
- In contrast to U.S. practice, defendants were permitted to give unsworn statements at the end of the trial.
- Hearsay evidence was allowed. This often came in the form of statements by individuals not called as witnesses. The statements were read by prosecutors; defendants, on cross-examination, were asked to respond to incriminating allegations. In U.S. courts, unlike at Nuremberg, the accused have the right to confront and question their accuser. At Nuremberg, evidence merely had to be "probative" to be admitted.
- The London Charter did not create a right to a jury trial.
- There was no right to appeal and no court to which the defendants could appeal. The defendants could ask the Control Council of Germany—the Allied occupation government, to reduce or change their sentences, and those who were found guilty did seek clemency from the Control Council. Their request

was rejected and ten of the eleven defendants who received death sentences were hanged two weeks later. (The eleventh, Hermann Goering, committed suicide several hours before he was to be hanged.)

- The defendants had a right to an attorney of their choice, although they could represent themselves if they wanted (none chose to do so). The four prosecuting nations paid the attorneys' fees.
- The defendants also had a right to present evidence in their own defense and to cross-examine any witnesses against them.
- The law of the London Charter was arguably ex post facto.

3

Defining Crimes Against Humanity

Encyclopedia of the Holocaust

The Allies did not decide to try the Nazis only for their mistreatment of the Jews, Gypsies, homosexuals, or others who were sent to the concentration camps. The principal motivation for the trial was to punish the leading Nazis for waging a war that cost the lives of 57 million people and wreaked untold devastation on most of Europe and parts of Africa, Asia, and the Middle East. There was little doubt that the crimes against peace would be sufficient to find the defendants at Nuremberg guilty; nevertheless, the Allies felt compelled to create a new charge that would make it possible to prosecute the Nazis for the atrocities they committed against civilians. The hope was that by demonstrating that these acts were considered crimes subject to prosecution, those inclined toward similar behavior in the future would be deterred. This entry from the *Encyclopedia of the Holocaust* defines the charge of "Crimes Against Humanity" and discusses some of the implications of its inclusion in the Nuremberg Trials.

A rticle 6 of the charter of the International Military Tribunal (IMT), which was to conduct the Nuremberg trial, empowered the IMT to try the major war criminals of the European Axis countries for three categories of crimes: crimes against peace, war crimes, and crimes against humanity.

Among the crimes defined as war crimes were violations of the laws or customs of war, such as murder, ill-treatment,

From "Crimes Against Humanity" entry in *Encyclopedia of the Holocaust*, vol. 1, edited by Israel Gutman (New York: Macmillan Library Reference, 1990). Reprinted by permission of The Gale Group.

deportation, forced labor, or wanton destruction not justified by military necessity. The IMT found that such acts, including also ill-treatment of civilian populations and prisoners of war, had been committed by the Fuhrer and his cohorts in total disregard of the fundamental principles of international law, and had been based instead on cold-blooded, criminal considerations. The IMT therefore decided to deal with the entire category of war crimes in great detail and to determine the individual defendants' guilt for such crimes. Included in the tribunal's deliberations were acts of murder and ill-treatment of prisoners of war and civilian populations, especially the persecution of Jews.

Such acts of persecution were also defined as crimes against humanity, even if they were committed before the war but were connected to preparations for the war. Article 6 (c) of the IMT charter defines crimes against humanity as "murder, extermination, enslavement, deportation, and other inhumane acts committed against any civilian population, before or during the war; or persecution on political, racial, or religious grounds in execution of or in connection with any crime within the jurisdiction of the tribunal, whether or not in violation of the domestic law of the country where perpetrated." It follows from this that the IMT was empowered to try crimes against humanity only if they were perpetrated in the execution of or in connection with war crimes or crimes against peace. Some of the acts defined as war crimes—such as murder, ill-treatment, and deportation—were also defined as crimes against humanity. These acts, however, were deemed war crimes only when they were a violation of the laws and customs of war, affecting the rights of fighting forces and the civilian population in occupied territory or in the course of warlike actions. Crimes against humanity, on the other hand, were defined as applying to acts against any civilian population—including the population of the country that commits the acts, and commits them on its own soil—at any time, in times of peace as well as in times of war. The latter feature—application to acts committed both in times of peace and times of war—also appears in the definition of crimes against peace, a category that includes not only the initiation and conduct of war, but also acts committed in times of peace, such as planning and preparation of aggression.

Crimes Against Humanity, Peace, and the International Community

The Unique Status of Crimes Against Humanity. A corollary of this is that it is neither the time in which the act is committed nor the act itself that constitutes the exclusive characteristic of a crime against humanity and sets it apart from the other crimes defined in the IMT charter. What distinguishes crimes against humanity from other crimes are the extraordinary brutality and diversity of means that the Nazis employed to commit these crimes, the unprecedented policy of persecution and extermination on which they were based, and the fact that while initially they were related to a policy of aggression, they exceeded by far the definition of war crimes in the traditional sense. Among the victims of the Nazi crimes against humanity were populations for which the laws and customs of war provide no protection— such as nationals of neutral countries, stateless persons, nationals of countries that were partners in the Axis, and, of course, nationals of Germany itself. Above all, most of the victims of the Nazi crimes against humanity were Jews, who, prior to the Nuremberg Trial, were not deemed to have protection based on international law.

Relation to War Crimes and Crimes Against Peace. There is some substance to the view that the introduction of the category of crimes against humanity was designed to serve as a support to the categories of war crimes and crimes against peace, or to cover a side effect related to these two categories. Crimes against humanity related to acts committed in times of peace as well, in the framework of planning and preparation for war, and on the territory of the aggressor or any other territory (not necessarily Nazi-occupied areas), against the aggressors' own nationals, the nationals of countries that were not at war with Germany, or stateless persons. Since these acts were related to preparations for war, the persons responsible for them could not be convicted under the laws and customs of war, which deal with situations involving actual warfare. The separate category of crimes against humanity also seeks to take into account another element: while the crimes to which it refers affect various populations—groups that were persecuted on national, racial, and religious grounds—the crimes all have in common the element of "inhumanity": the cruel methods that were employed, and the unprecedented purpose of mass extermination of victims simply for belonging to a certain group (or being classified, by the criminals, as belonging to that group), without the victims' having committed any offense whatsoever.

A Crime Against the International Community. Every crime is an offense not only against the victim, but also against the established order of the country in which it takes place—the country as a social organization that includes all its citizens, irrespective of color, political views, and origin. Similarly, every international crime, especially when it is a crime against humanity, is an attack on the international community as a whole, threatening the safeguards of its peace, and indeed its very existence. Nevertheless, what distinguishes crimes against humanity from the other categories of crimes is their "inhumanity," rather than the injury they inflict upon "humanity" as a worldwide community; this was why they were designated as crimes against "humanity" in the abstract sense of the term. However, acts defined as crimes against peace or war crimes can also be regarded as crimes against humanity, since the planning and carrying out of aggression prepares the conditions for inhumane offenses against human rights.

Legal Precedents—Hague and Geneva Conventions. The element of humanity and the condemnation of and punishment for inhumane acts are not recent innovations in international law, the dictates of human conscience having long been regarded as one of international law's sources. Thus, the Petersburg Declaration of 1868 stated that the dictates of humanity must take precedence over the needs of war; and the fourth Hague Convention (1907) specified that in situations not specifically provided for in the convention, the civilian population and the fighting forces would also be protected by the principles of humanity and the dictates of society's conscience. This principle has since been reconfirmed time and again in various international treaties and conventions, such as the 1949 Geneva Convention and the 1977 Supplementary Protocols.

The IMT extended this principle to apply also to criminal acts that are not war crimes, in order to provide protection to every civilian population and to every individual, irrespective of his nationality and his country's policy and laws. Evidently, the principle is valid under all circumstances and takes precedence over every national law and every bilateral or multilateral international agreement; it is a universal and cogent principle, which is not subject to challenge and cannot be deviated from by unilateral decision; it can be changed or replaced only by a humanitarian principle that is of an even higher order (as stated in the 1969 Vienna Convention on Treaties). This means that, in formal terms, the definition of inhumane acts as being criminal in nature does not depend on the legal system or established policy of the country in which such acts occur. In this respect, too, crimes against humanity are sui generis, different from other criminal acts.

A Crime of a Different Order. The criminal nature of crimes against humanity is far worse and of a totally different order than that of any other criminal act defined as such by the criminal codes of all civilized nations. This criminal practice was demonstrated in its most radical form by the Nazi policy and acts of brutal mass murder and extermination of entire peoples and population groups. The unique character of a crime against humanity can also be recognized in other acts that in the European continental system of law have long been classified as inherently criminal (*malum per se*), and that in Soviet legal terminology constitute a threat to society and public order.

Political Acts?

Opponents to the Nuremberg Judgement. These aspects of crimes against humanity and crimes against peace are disregarded by those who have challenged the justice and the very nature of the Nuremberg Trial because it included these categories in the stated principles upon which it based the indictment. Such acts, so their argument goes, were political acts, for which those who committed them cannot be held accountable, as heads of sovereign entities who were not subject to any other entity or to any law other than a law declared as valid by their own state. It is true that in a certain respect the crimes defined by the IMT charter are of a political character, since their planning, preparation, and execution were possible only in the framework of operations, guidelines, initiatives, and decrees emanating from and authorized by the political administration of a state. This, however, is no reason to treat the persons responsible for these crimes as political criminals in the accepted sense of that term, since their acts were linked to the theory of racism and to other inhumane concepts that have no precedent in the annals of mankind. Thus it was declared, in legal theory and practice, that such criminals may be tried by any country that does not want to, or has no reason to, extradite them for trial in other countries or by international tribunals.

Furthermore, their status is like that of other categories of criminals to whom the principle of universal jurisdiction and punishment applies. Nor may these criminals seek to justify their acts by claiming that they were performing their official duties or acting on orders from their superiors. One restriction that the IMT charter did impose was that in order for crimes against humanity to be tried, they had to be related to war crimes or crimes against peace, either as side effects of such crimes or in support of them.

Many legal experts and human-rights activists seek to abolish this restrictive condition in the codification of international criminal law. They point out that while this condition applied to those tried at the Nuremberg Trial and the Tokyo trial of major Japanese war criminals, it should not be applicable to other criminals charged with crimes against humanity, and consequently their prosecution should not be linked to war crimes or crimes against peace. Indeed, such a link is conspicuous by its absence in Allied Control Council Law No. 10, of December 20, 1945, and in the laws of other countries, among them Israel's Nazis and Nazi Collaborators (Punishment) Law 5710-1950.

The Nuremberg Trial as a Precedent. It is true that in most of the trials the Allies held in their zones of occupation in Germany, the judges preferred to follow the IMT precedent and held defendants responsible for crimes against humanity only when the acts were committed in the preparation of aggression or in violation of the laws and customs of war. This was so in the subsequent Nuremberg proceedings, held by the Americans, in which the Nuremberg Military Tribunals tried Nazi judges, industrialists, and Einsatzgruppen personnel, among others. Those who call for the complete separation of the concept of crimes against humanity from war crimes and crimes against peace do so in order to endow this concept with the status of a human-rights principle that would protect all human beings at all times and under all conditions, completely independent of warlike events.

4

Four Powers, Four Opinions on Procedure

Ann Tusa and John Tusa

Once the British, Russians, Americans, and French agreed to hold a trial, the four powers still had to decide many crucial issues regarding the procedure for the trial, the charges against the defendants, and even the site of the tribunal. These were all contentious issues. The head of the American delegation, Robert Jackson, had definite ideas about how the trial should be run and expected the others to go along. The British, who shared a similar legal system, were inclined to agree with most of Jackson's suggestions, but the Russians and French had different legal traditions and preferred to include elements they were more comfortable with in the conduct of the trial. The Russians were particularly obstinate on many issues and had agreed to a trial to begin with because they presumed it would simply announce punishments for the Nazis. This was completely at odds with Jackson's determination that Nuremberg not be a "show trial." This excerpt by Ann Tusa, a history teacher, and her journalist husband John Tusa, describes some of the negotiations conducted at a conference in London by the lawyers in preparing for the trial.

Judge Jackson . . . certainly would not accept anything that smacked of a show trial. On the day of Roosevelt's death, he told the American Society of International Law in Washington that it was better to shoot Nazi criminals out of hand after a military or political decision than to destroy belief in judicial process by conducting farcical trials. True trials must be based on the clear traditions of justice, must follow the principles and methods universally adopted by those with respect for the law. 'You must put no man on trial before anything that is called a court . . . under forms of judicial proceeding, if you are not willing to see him freed if not proved guilty. If you are determined to execute a man in any case, there is no occasion for a trial; the world yields no respect to courts that are merely organized to convict.'. . .

Nikitchenko did not want a trial, merely formal confirmation of political decision.

Many of the basic issues in the trial were already clear in Jackson's mind. The 'crime which comprehends all lesser crimes is the crime of making unjustifiable war.' International law had thrown 'a mantle of protection around acts which otherwise would be crimes, when committed in pursuit of legitimate warfare': killings, destruction, oppression. He was not worried about a lack of precedents or the absence of legislation: international law must grow 'as did the Common Law, through decisions reached from time to time and adapting settled principles to new situations.' Nor had he any doubts that pre-war treaties and agreements had made aggressive war a crime; and 'it is high time we act on the judicial principle that aggressive war-making is illegal and criminal.' There could be no accepting claims that heads of state are immune from legal liability: American citizens could bring their officials before courts; this right should be available in the international sphere. Nor should leading officials and military men be allowed the defence that they bear no guilt for carrying out orders from their superiors. Let them show the facts about those orders, then leave judges to decide whether they were illegal and to what extent they might constitute extenuating circumstance. 'We do not accept the paradox that legal responsibility should be least where the power is the greatest,' said Jackson. . . .

The British talked more of practicalities than the cause of establishing the rule of international law. They were anxious to name the defendants, limit the scope of the trial, whereas Jackson talked of general aims and charges and in a memo stressed the need to authenticate the whole history of Nazism and show its criminal design. All this, however, did not seem significant enough to ruffle Jackson's confidence. The British War Crimes Executive was keen on the principle of a trial and he was certain his draft proposals would only require minor modifications to ensure their full agreement.

Jackson's troubles began with the arrival of the French negotiators on 24 June and the Russians on the 25th. Both groups must have suspected that the Americans and the British had been ganging up on them in their absence. . . .

The French team was led by Robert Falco of the Cour de Cassation. Patrick Dean of the Foreign Office, who was an observer at the conference, found him 'rather a nonentity.'. . .

The Russians were led by General Nikitchenko, Vice-Chairman of the Soviet Supreme Court and one-time lecturer in criminal law at the Academy of Military Jurisprudence in Moscow. . . .

The French and the Russians were not men to be steam rollered; Jackson could not expect them to sit quietly and accept every American suggestion with a nod. They had views of their own, and convictions as strong as his, but sometimes different. What was disturbing for him, too, was that they represented the Continental legal tradition based on the Roman Law which he seems to have encountered in London for the first time. With the British, Jackson had colleagues whose reactions stemmed from the same Common Law assumptions, whose procedures and principles were very similar to those of American lawyers. With the French and Russians, however, he faced a different mentality, not conditioned by the Common Law and indeed potentially critical or even hostile to some of its bases. . . .

Lawyers as Diplomats

A high proportion of the time at the Conference was spent on procedural matters—working out how the trial should be run, what should happen when, who should have what powers. All were agreed that a military rather than a civil tribunal would free them to pool the best elements from all their national systems. Since they were embarking on a totally new enterprise they need not be hidebound by previously established procedures. For instance, they could ignore the rules of evidence which normally applied in trials with juries and allow the Tribunal to admit any evidence which seemed to have probative value—provided it was clearly relevant to the point it was substantiating and was not repetitious. All were agreed they could create a new court procedure for the occasion which must be efficient and fair. The trouble was they could not then agree on how to do it. All tended to cling to the conviction that their own national way of doing things was best. . . .

There were arguments too over the role of the judges. The French and Russians wanted their familiar system where judges intervene frequently to direct the course of the trial and examine defendants and witnesses. The British and Americans were more accustomed to the adversary process of challenge and cross-examination by opposing counsel. The Continental delegates also wanted to insist on the right of defendants to speak when not under oath and to make a final speech in their own defence.

The Charter expressed the eventual happy union between the Common Law and the Continental systems of procedure.

It was certainly arguable that the Continental court procedure would be acceptable to half the judges in an international tribunal and undoubtedly more familiar to German defendants. It proved difficult, however, to combine elements of it with those aspects of common law procedure on which the Americans and British insisted. . . .

Nikitchenko had thrown a bombshell by suddenly announcing: 'We are dealing here with the chief war criminals who have already been condemned and whose conviction has already been announced by both the Moscow and Crimea Declarations by the heads of government.' The Tribunal's job was simply to announce 'just punishment for the offences which have been committed.' So presumably Nikitchenko did not want a trial, merely formal confirmation of political decision; saw no need for a careful examination of the evidence; thought the rights of defendants to be nothing more than an impediment to speedy punishment.

That is certainly what Jackson assumed. He leapt to defend his belief in a true trial. Amazingly calm and coherent under such provocation he insisted that the political declarations had been an accusation, not a conviction; 'if we are going to have a trial then it must be an actual trial.' He laid it firmly on the line that the Americans 'would not be parties to setting up a mere formal judicial body to ratify a political decision to convict'—the judges must 'inquire into the evidence and reach an independent decision.'. . . .

Nikitchenko's statement had undoubtedly shattered Jackson's assumption that Russian presence at the Conference implied acceptance of the basic principles of his scheme for a trial. It had also suggested a willingness to ride roughshod over the normal standards of justice. It must have created a deep suspicion in Jackson's mind that the Russians lacked any commitment to true legality. . . .

This unshakeable determination that a trial of major Nazi leaders must be based on the norms of justice and on sound legal practice lay at the heart of the crucial confrontation of the London delegates over the fundamental issue of whether the defendants should be charged with launching wars of aggression. Jackson saw the charge of aggressive war as the cornerstone of the case against the Nazi regime, the 'central point of the show' as his son described it. From this crime stemmed the others. The French too believed that the charge was 'morally and politically desirable.' The trouble was they did not think it was legal. . . .

Nikitchenko agreed—he thought the United Nations must reach a decision on the criminality of aggression and that until they had defined it others must not pre-empt them. He and the French were only prepared to charge the defendants with specific acts of breaking treaties and invasions, 'deemed criminal,' and leave it to the judges to decide the law which covered them. . . .

The only American plan which was not discussed exhaustively day after day at the Conference was the intention to charge the Nazi leaders with conspiracy, the essential bond of the Bernays plan. The conspiracy charge, as Jackson argued at London, was to deal only with 'those who deliberately entered a plan aimed at forbidden acts' not with the millions of soldiers, or the farmers who occasionally employed slave labour at harvest time. He wanted to reach 'the planners, the zealots who put this thing across.' These were the people the British, French and Russians wanted to reach too. They just did not think that the American concept of conspiracy was the way to do it. The charge was little discussed at their main sessions—while it endured death by a thousand cuts in the drafting sub-committee. In draft and redraft, conspiracy was either omitted altogether, or it was whittled away to an accusation of 'planning' or 'organizing' specific crimes.

The British might take the American concept for granted, but their pragmatism suggested its use was too vague, too grandiose to be effective in court. The Russians and French were accustomed to the idea that conspiring to commit crimes is illegal, but in their law the concentration must be on the criminal act itself. Given their experience of invasion and occupation in recent years, it seemed only too obvious that the Nazis had committed crimes and that these crimes had been planned and supervised by their leaders. Why, then, bother to make planning, for which conspiracy only seemed a fancy word, a separate charge? There was evidence in plenty to prove the top Nazis committed actual crimes.

Why Nuremberg?

Jackson had to face much more argument over what might have seemed a straightforward question—where the international tribunal should be established. Jackson wanted an early decision so that work could start on preparing a prison for the defendants and many of the witnesses, a courtroom, accommodation for the judges, barristers and their staffs as well as for the numerous journalists and visitors who could be expected. A multitude of facilities would be needed for feeding those present, giving them communications with the outside world, for storage, duplication and circulation of the thousands of sheets of record and printed documentary evidence. It would be a major logistical task at any period. In the rubble of a starving Germany—where everyone was agreed the trial must take place—it was a herculean one. The US Army had advised Jackson that Berlin was already overcrowded and its resources overstretched. He visited Munich whose ruins offered little possibility for staging a trial. General Clay, however, recommended Nuremberg. Although Allied bombing had reduced the city to the point where 90 per cent of it was officially termed 'dead,' by a miracle certain essentials had escaped destruction. Jackson went to look. He reported to the Conference that the courtroom in the Palace of Justice at Nuremberg 'is not as large as it ought to be, perhaps, but it is larger than any other courtroom standing,' and 'the jail facilities are very adequate' (1,200 prisoners could be accommodated) and linked directly to the court. There was enough office space in the Palace of Justice and possible billetting in the suburbs—all in need of repair, but at least reparable in a country virtually bereft of building materials.

Added to these advantages were other attractions. Nuremberg had symbolic significance. It was the scene of the huge Nazi Rallies, the promulgation of the infamous Laws against the Jews. Not least—it was in the American zone. American rations were notoriously better than anyone else's in 1945; the Americans had the money, the access to equipment, the 'can do' for the construction work and the provision of adequate comforts for a major international event. The British and French were delighted with the offer. The Russians were not. Nikitchenko insisted that the trial must be held in Berlin. So keen was he on Berlin he even described it as 'central.' His best argument was that it was jointly run by the Four Powers, which made it fitting for an international tribunal; he thought the Allied Control Commission could provide the necessary back-up personnel (the ACC was less certain). It was clear to the others, though, that Berlin was an island in the Russian sector. The trial would be dependent on the Russians for rations and communications—and Russians were not famous for comfortable living or efficiency. Jackson must have raised their hearts talking about installing central heating; their hearts must have sunk again as Nikitchenko disputed the need for heating in the early months of the winter—even in the mornings, as Jackson recommended. Jackson offered everyone a trip in his plane to see Nuremberg. At the last moment, the Russians refused to go.

Everyone else went and was impressed. Gradually they wore the Russians down into accepting Nuremberg as the site of the trial on condition that Berlin was named the 'permanent seat of the Tribunal' and that the judges met there first. . . .

The Charter

On 8 August the heads of delegation in London signed two documents which they had been working on at the suggestion of the Russians from the earliest stages of the Conference. The first was a statement of the general intention to fulfil the wishes of the United Nations and the signatories of the Moscow Declaration. This London Agreement announced the intention to establish an International Military Tribunal 'for the trial of war criminals whose offences have no particular geographical location, whether they be accused individually or in their capacity as members of organizations or groups or in both capacities.' Nineteen other nations later expressed their adherence to this London Agreement. . . .

The Charter expressed the eventual happy union between the Common Law and Continental systems of procedure. As everyone had wished, the accused were given the right to counsel, and to an indictment and trial in their own language. As a compromise between the two systems the defendants would be served in advance of the trial with an indictment which gave a full summary of the evidence against them and which was accompanied with as many of the relevant documents as possible; others could then be produced in court and time given to the defence to study them. The Tribunal might decide to have evidence taken by Masters on commission, but, thanks to Russian insistence, these Masters were only to take statements, they could not make recommendations to the court, as Jackson had wished. Defendants would have the right to take the stand and testify under oath, subject to cross-examination (which is not usual on the Continent); and to make a final statement without prosecution challenge and not under oath (a right unfamiliar in Anglo-American courts). The result of the blend of two systems was, in Jackson's view, to give rather more rights to the defendants than might have been available in either system separately. . . .

Individual defendants and organizations were to be heard on three counts. The first was the crime of planning and waging aggressive war. It had been given a new name—previously coined by Professor Trainin—Crimes against Peace. In view of the doubts of the French and Russians as to the status of aggressive war in international law, it was not given a general definition, and the introduction to the charge made it clear that the Tribunal was empowered only to try and punish those who acted in the interests of 'the European Axis Powers.' This was an undoubted defeat for Jackson who had so longed for the chance to show that any war was criminal. But he put the best face he could on the situation in a Press release which stated: 'If we can cultivate in the world the idea that aggressive war-making is the way to the prisoner's dock rather than to honours, we will have accomplished something to make the peace more secure.' The Charter had created a minor problem for him as the leader of a prosecution team, however. In defining a crime against peace as the waging of war, it had probably ruled out reference by the prosecution to the takeover of Austria in the Anschluss or the invasion of Czechoslovakia, since in those cases no actual fighting had occurred. Law Ten of the Allied Control Council cleared this up for subsequent proceedings by talking of wars *and* invasions.

The Charter had established the outlines for a trial of the Nazi leaders, but it left many of the important details to be settled by their judges.

In the deliberately created murk of the wording on conspiracy it seemed the Nazi leaders would be held to account for planning Crimes against Peace. However, it was far from clear that they would have to answer for planning the other two forms of criminal activity in the Charter, as Jackson had wished. Count Two dealt with War Crimes. At first glance this charge was less novel than Crimes against Peace. The Charter's definition of War Crimes followed that of firmly established international agreements; war criminals had frequently been prosecuted and punished for these crimes. It was however an innovation to suggest that responsibility for these criminal activities ultimately rested with those who governed or commanded those who engaged them. . . .

The final Count in the Charter—that of Crimes against Humanity—was a totally new charge. The name first coined at Versailles was recommended to the Conference by Professor Hersch Lauterpacht to cover the persecution of racial and religious groups and the wholesale exploitation of European people and resources. Perhaps many of the acts covered by this charge could have been included in the list of war crimes. But existing laws did not always envisage the nature and scale of the atrocities which had been committed. Nor could the charge of War Crimes be stretched to deal with, for example, the attempted extermination of Ger-

man Jews. The charge of Crimes against Humanity expressed the revulsion against Nazi attitudes and methods
which had been so strongly felt by those who drew up the
Charter. As lawyers, however, some of them had felt scru-
ples about the right of an international court to interfere in
the domestic polity of a sovereign state. Strong though the
temptation had been to prosecute German leaders for persecuting the Jews, the Christian churches, and political opponents in the 1930s, the Charter resisted it. Persecutions
had to be examined 'in connection with any crimes within
the jurisdiction of the Tribunal.' This strongly suggested
that they must be directly connected with the War and
probably had to be committed after 1939. Jackson would
have a hard job to convince the Tribunal of his belief that
they were all deliberately part of the entire Nazi design
right from the beginning of the regime.

No such problems of limitations hedged Article Eight
of the Charter which made clear that no defendant could
claim the protection of having obeyed orders from a superior, though superior orders might be considered by the
Tribunal as a mitigating factor in sentencing. The denial of
the defence of superior orders has often been called the
'Nuremberg Principle.' It was not, however, new at the trial.
It was perfectly familiar in national legal systems—and, indeed, it was probably even more familiar to the German
military than to anyone. Every German soldier's paybook
contained 'Ten Commandments' one of which stated that
no soldier should obey an illegal order. . . .

Clear though the Charter might be on questions such as
this, it was in fact riddled with unanswered questions; not
least, what was the law on aggressive war? Had the Nazis
planned to commit crimes other than launching war; if so,
from what date? What makes a man a conspirator? Can declarations of criminality against organizations be made and
then be binding on subsequent courts? Nor had the framers
of the Charter chosen to impose many rules on the Tribunal
for handling the case in court.

It might have been expected that the signatories of the
London Agreement would have invented the game, evolved
rules for playing it which gave the advantage to one side
only, then gone out to play certain of victory. Instead, thanks
to lawyers' rectitude and national differences, the rule book
was vague, the options available to the players ill-defined but

not limited to one side, and even the size of the pitch was not specified. In this situation the referee can start to create much of the game. The Charter had established the outline for a trial of the Nazi leaders, but it left many of the important details to be settled by their judges. Through their analysis of the law and the interpretation of the sketch they had been given for the trial, by the way they chose to use the powers given to them and by the rules they evolved for controlling the process, they could shape it and largely determine its outcome. This was going to be very much a trial held by the judges, not one staged by the prosecution. The negotiators at the London Conference had all been agreed on one thing—that the case against the Nazi leaders was open and shut; they would all be found guilty and punished. Whether they now realized it or not, though, the Charter had taken the initiative from the prosecution and given it to the judges. A walkover victory for the prosecution was no longer guaranteed.

It might well be argued that this very failure to build in a guarantee of prosecution success was one of the great strengths of the Charter—even if it was not one of its intended virtues. . . .

A Popular Decision

Few of the questions they raised, philosophical or practical, troubled the public at large in August 1945. Some of them were highly technical and only appreciated by lawyers. Some of them would only become apparent during the trial itself. The Agreement and Charter were universally welcomed by the Press. The *New York Herald Tribune* acclaimed the Charter as 'a great and historic document, an essential companion piece to the Charter of the United Nations.' All papers spotted—as the *Glasgow Herald* put it—that 'the court is new and so are the charges.' All of them too, like the *New York Times*, welcomed 'a new code of international morals' in the Charter. Lawyers might wince at acting without precedent. Press and public alike in 1945 were delighted by innovation. In the post-war mood men were looking for a new and better world; new, they thought, would undoubtedly be better than the old. As the *New York Times* put it, 'these are not days in which the people of the world are inclined to quibble over precedents. There must sometimes be a beginning.'

No one questioned the desirability of a trial. Like *The Times* they called on the 'Grand Assize' at Nuremberg 'to record the solemn abjuration by the general conscience of the supreme offences against humanity (by the Nazis), to vindicate the effective reality of the law of nations and to leave to posterity a supreme warning of the fate of the guilty.' Least of all did any newspaper question the right of the victorious powers to conduct it. The Press had already condemned the Nazi regime. They might welcome a full judicial procedure and the right of the accused to defend themselves, but everyone would agree with the *New York Times* that: 'Most of the people of the world would judge it poor justice if the men who brought about this war were to escape their punishment.'

In his statement to the Press on the signing of the London Agreement, Jackson tried to preempt any criticism of the victors trying the defeated Germans. He feared the trial would be seen as the victor wreaking vengeance on the vanquished. But 'however unfortunate it may be, there seems no way of doing anything about the crimes against peace and against humanity except that the victors judge the vanquished.' The questions of victory or defeat were in fact irrelevant. 'We must make it clear to the Germans that the wrong for which their fallen leaders are on trial is not that they lost the War, but that they started it.'

5

The Chief Prosecutor's Opening Speech

Robert Jackson

The opening statement in a criminal trial is usually designed to give an overview of the prosecution's case, explain the reason for the prosecution, highlight the evidence, and foreshadow the links that will be made between the crimes and the defendants. Chief counsel Robert Jackson had an awesome responsibility in his opening statement because the eyes of the world were on Nuremberg, waiting to see if the Nazis would be punished for their actions and if they could be tried with any measure of impartiality. Jackson clearly understood his role and adroitly explained the importance of the case in the context of world affairs; however, he also made the point that this prosecution had some similarities to more common trials in which individuals seek to evade responsibility either by claiming that they were simply following orders or that they had no direct involvement in the crime. In the following excerpts from his speech, Jackson gives an excellent overview of the charges and the evidence, confronts many of the objections to the trial and challenges to its legal underpinnings, and, perhaps most important, argues forcefully that no one should be above the law. Jackson was a legal scholar who was appointed to the Supreme Court by President Roosevelt in 1941. He took a leave of absence to serve as chief prosecutor at the Nuremberg Trial.

The wrongs which we seek to condemn and punish have been so calculated, so malignant, and so devastating, that civilization cannot tolerate their being ignored, because

From the opening speech of Robert Jackson, November 21, 1945, in *Trial of the Major War Criminals Before the International Military Tribunal*, vol. 2: *Proceedings, November 14–30, 1945* (Nuremberg: International Military Tribunal, 1947).

it cannot survive their being repeated. That four great nations, flushed with victory and stung with injury stay the hand of vengeance and voluntarily submit their captive enemies to the judgment of the law is one of the most significant tributes that Power has ever paid to Reason.

This Tribunal, while it is novel and experimental, is not the product of abstract speculations nor is it created to vindicate legalistic theories. This inquest represents the practical effort of four of the most mighty of nations, with the support of 17 more, to utilize international law to meet the greatest menace of our times—aggressive war. The common sense of mankind demands that law shall not stop with the punishment of petty crimes by little people. It must also reach men who possess themselves of great power and make deliberate and concerted use of it to set in motion evils which leave no home in the world untouched. It is a cause of that magnitude that the United Nations will lay before Your Honors. . . .

Unfortunately the nature of these crimes is such that both prosecution and judgment must be by victor nations over vanquished foes. The worldwide scope of the aggressions carried out by these men has left but few real neutrals. Either the victors must judge the vanquished or we must leave the defeated to judge themselves. After the first World War, we learned the futility of the latter course. The former high station of these defendants, the notoriety of their acts, and the adaptability of their conduct to provoke retaliation make it hard to distinguish between the demand for a just and measured retribution, and the unthinking cry for vengeance which arises from the anguish of war. It is our task, so far as humanly possible, to draw the line between the two. We must never forget that the record on which we judge these defendants today is the record on which history will judge us tomorrow. . . .

If these men are the first war leaders of a defeated nation to be prosecuted in the name of the law, they are also the first to be given a chance to plead for their lives in the name of the law. . . . They do have a fair opportunity to defend themselves—a favor which these men, when in power, rarely extended to their fellow countrymen. Despite the fact that public opinion already condemns their acts, we agree that here they must be given a presumption of innocence and we accept the burden of proving criminal acts and the responsibility of these defendants for their commission. . . .

The Nazi conspiracy, as we shall show, always contemplated not merely overcoming current opposition but exterminating elements which could not be reconciled with its philosophy of the state. It not only sought to establish the Nazi "new order" but to secure its sway, as Hitler predicted, "for a thousand years." Nazis were never in doubt or disagreement as to what these dissident elements were. They were concisely described by one of the Colonel General Von Fritsch, on 12/11/1938 in these words:

> Shortly after the first war I came to the conclusion that we would have to be victorious in three battles if Germany were to become powerful again: 1. The battle against the working class—Hitler has won this. 2. Against the Catholic Church, perhaps better expressed against Ultramontanism. 3. Against the Jews. . . .

The Battle Against the Working Class

When Hitler came to power, there were in Germany three groups of trade unions. The General German Trade Union Confederation (ADGB) with 28 affiliated unions, and the General Independent Employees Confederation (AFA) with 13 federated unions together numbered more than 4.5 million members. The Christian Trade Union had over 1.25 million members.

The working people of Germany, like the working people of other nations, had little to gain personally by war. . . .

The first Nazi attack was upon the two larger unions. . . .

All funds of the labor unions, including pension and benefit funds, were seized [on 5/2/1933]. Union leaders were sent to concentration camps. A few days later, on 5/10/1933, Hitler appointed Robert Ley leader of the German Labor Front (Deutsche Arbeitsfront). . . . The Party order provided that "outside of the German Labor Front, no other organization (whether of workers or of employees) is to exist." On 6/24/1933 the remaining Christian Trade Unions were seized, pursuant to an order of the Nazi Party signed by Ley.

On 5/19/1933, this time by a government decree, it was provided that "trustees" of labor appointed by Hitler, should regulate the conditions of all labor contracts, replacing the former process of collective bargaining. On 11/30/1934 a decree "regulating national labor" introduced the Fuehrer Principle into industrial relations. It provided that the owners of enterprises should be the "Fuehrer" and the workers should be the followers. The "enterprise-Fuehrer" should "make decisions for employees and laborers in all matters concerning the enterprise." It was by such bait that the great German industrialists were induced to support the Nazi cause, to their own ultimate ruin.

Not only did the Nazis dominate and regiment German labor but they forced the youth into the ranks of the laboring people thus led into chains. Under a compulsory labor service decree on 6/26/1935 young men and women between the ages of 18–25 were conscripted for labor. . . . The productive manpower of the German nation was in Nazi control. By these steps the defendants won the battle to liquidate labor unions as potential opposition and were enabled to impose upon the working class the burdens of preparing for aggressive warfare. . . .

The Battle Against the Churches

The Nazi Party always was predominantly anti-Christian in its ideology. But we who believe in freedom of conscience and of religion base no charge of criminality on anybody's ideology. It is not because the Nazis themselves were irreligious or pagan, but because they persecuted others of the Christian faith that they become guilty of crime, and it is because the persecution was a step in the preparation for aggressive warfare that the offense becomes one of international consequence. To remove every moderating influence among the German people and to put its population on a total war footing, the conspirators devised and carried out a systematic and relentless repression of all Christian sects and churches.

We will ask you to convict the Nazis on their own evidence. Martin Bormann, in 6/1941, issued a secret decree on the relation of Christianity and National Socialism. The decree provided:

> For the first time in German history the Fuehrer consciously and completely has the leadership of the people in his own hand. With the Party, its components, and attached units the Fuehrer has created for himself and thereby the German Reich leadership an instrument which makes him independent of the

church. All influences which might impair or damage the leadership of the people exercised by the Fuehrer with help of the NSDAP, must be eliminated. More and more the people must be separated from the churches and their organs, the pastors. Of course, the churches must and will, seen from their viewpoint, defend themselves against this loss of power. But never again must an influence on leadership of the people be yielded to the churches. This (influence) must be broken completely and finally.

Only the Reich Government and by its direction the Party, its components, and attached units have a right to leadership of the people. Just as the deleterious influences of astrologers, seers, and other fakers are eliminated and suppressed by the State, so must the possibility of church influence also be totally removed. Not until this has happened, does the State leadership have influence on the individual citizens. Not until then are people and Reich secure in their existence for all the future. . . .

Crimes Against the Jews

The most savage and numerous crimes planned and committed by the Nazis were those against the Jews. Those in Germany in 1933 numbered about 500,000. In the aggregate, they had made for themselves positions which excited envy, and had accumulated properties which excited the avarice of the Nazis. They were few enough to be helpless and numerous enough to be held up as a menace.

Let there be no misunderstanding about the charge of persecuting Jews. What we charge against these defendants is not those arrogances and pretensions which frequently accompany the intermingling of different peoples and which are likely, despite the honest efforts of government, to produce regrettable crimes and convulsions. It is my purpose to show a plan and design, to which all Nazis were fanatically committed, to annihilate all Jewish people. These crimes were organized and promoted by the Party leadership, executed and protected by the Nazi officials, as we shall convince you by written orders of the Secret State Police itself.

The persecution of the Jews was a continuous and deliberate policy. It was a policy directed against other nations as well as against the Jews themselves. Anti-Semitism was promoted to divide and embitter the democratic peoples and to soften their resistance to the Nazi aggression. . . .

The Nazi Party always was predominately anti-Christian in its ideology.

The persecution policy against the Jews commenced with nonviolent measures such as disfranchisement and discriminations against their religion, and the placing of impediments in the way of success in economic life. It moved rapidly to organized mass violence against them, physical isolation in ghettos, deportation, labor, mass starvation, and extermination. The Government, the party formations indicted before you as criminal organizations, the Secret State Police, the Army, private and semi-public associations, and "spontaneous" mobs that were carefully inspired from official sources, were all agencies that were concerned in this persecution. Nor was it directed against individual Jews for personal bad citizenship or unpopularity. The avowed purpose was the destruction of the Jewish people as a whole, as an end in itself, as a measure of preparation for war, and as a discipline of conquered peoples.

The conspiracy or common plan to exterminate the Jew was so methodically and thoroughly pursued, that despite the German defeat and Nazi prostration this Nazi aim largely has succeeded. Only remnants of the European Jewish population remain in Germany, in the countries which Germany occupied, and in those which were her satellites or collaborators. Of the 9.6 million Jews who lived in Nazi-dominated Europe, 60% are authoritatively estimated to have perished. 5.7 million Jews are missing from the countries in which they formerly lived, and over 4.5 million cannot be accounted for by the normal death rate nor by immigration; nor are they included among displaced persons. History does not record a crime ever perpetrated against so many victims or one ever carried out with such calculated cruelty. . . .

The most serious of the actions against Jews were outside of any law, but the law itself was employed to some extent. There were the infamous Nuremberg decrees of 9/15/1935. The Jews were segregated into ghettos and put into forced labor; they were expelled from their professions; their property was expropriated; all cultural life, the press, the theater, and schools were prohibited them. . . .

As the German frontiers were expanded by war, so the campaign against the Jews expanded. The Nazi plan never was limited to extermination in Germany; always it contemplated extinguishing the Jew in Europe and often in the world. In the West, the Jews were killed and their property taken over. But the campaign achieved its zenith of savagery in the East. The eastern Jew has suffered as no people ever suffered. . . .

If I should recite these horrors in words of my own, you would think me intemperate and unreliable. Fortunately, we need not take the word of any witness but the Germans themselves. I invite you now to look at a few of the vast number of captured German orders and reports that will be offered in evidence, to see what a Nazi invasion meant. We will present such evidence as the report of Einsatzgruppe (Action Group) A of 10/15/1941 which boasts that in overrunning the Baltic States, "Native anti-Semitic forces were induced to start pogroms against the Jews during the first hours after occupation. . . ." The report continues:

> From the beginning it was to be expected that the Jewish problem in the East could not be solved by pogroms alone.
>
> In accordance with the basic orders received, however, the cleansing activities of the Security Police had to aim at a complete annihilation of the Jews. Special detachments reinforced by selected units—in Lithuania partisan detachments, in Latvia units of the Latvian auxiliary police—therefore performed extensive executions both in the towns and in rural areas. The actions of the execution detachments were performed smoothly.
>
> The sum total of the Jews liquidated in Lithuania amounts to 71,105. During the pogroms in Kovno 3800 Jews were eliminated, in the smaller towns about 1200 Jews. In Latvia, up to now a total of 30,000 Jews

were executed. Five hundred were eliminated by pogroms in Riga. . . .

There are reports which merely tabulate the numbers slaughtered. An example is an account of the work of Einsatzgruppen of SIPO and SD in the East, which relates that:

In Estonia all Jews were arrested immediately upon the arrival of the Wehrmacht. Jewish men and women above the age of 16 and capable of work were drafted for forced labor. Jews were subjected to all sorts of restrictions and all Jewish property was confiscated. All Jewish males above the age of 16 were executed, with the exception of doctors and elders. Only 500 of an original 4,500 Jews remained. Thirty-seven thousand, one hundred eighty persons have been liquidated by the SIPO and SD in White Ruthenia during October. In one town, 337 Jewish women were executed for demonstrating a 'provocative attitude.' In another, 380 Jews were shot for spreading vicious propaganda.

And so the report continues, listing town after town, where hundreds of Jews were murdered:

In Vitebsk 3000 Jews were liquidated because of the danger of epidemics. In Kiev 33,771 Jews were executed on September 29 and 30 in retaliation for some fires which were set off there. In Shitomir 3145 Jews 'had to be shot' because, judging from experience they had to be considered as the carriers of Bolshevik propaganda. In Cherson 410 Jews were executed in reprisal against acts of sabotage. In the territory east of the Dnieper, the Jewish problem was 'solved' by the liquidation of 4891 Jews and by putting the remainder into labor battalions of up to 1000 persons.

Other accounts tell not of the slaughter so much as of the depths of degradation to which the tormentors stooped. For example, we will show the report made to Defendant Rosenberg about the army and the SS in the area under Rosenberg's jurisdiction, which recited the following:

Details: In presence of SS man, a Jewish dentist has to break all gold teeth and fillings out of mouth of German and Russian Jews before they are executed.

Men, women and children are locked into barns and burned alive.

Peasants, women and children are shot on the pretext that they are suspected of belonging to bands. . . .

I shall not dwell on this subject longer than to quote one more sickening document which evidences the planned and systematic character of the Jewish persecutions. I hold a report written with Teutonic devotion to detail, illustrated with photographs to authenticate its almost incredible text, and beautifully bound in leather with the loving care bestowed on a proud work. It is the original report of the SS Brigadier General Stroop in charge of the destruction of the Warsaw Ghetto, and its title page carries the inscription "The Jewish ghetto in Warsaw no longer exists." It is characteristic that one of the captions explains that the photograph concerned shows the driving out of Jewish "bandits"; those whom the photograph shows being driven out are almost entirely women and little children. It contains a day-by-day account of the killings mainly carried out by the SS organization, too long to relate, but let me quote General Stroop's summary:

> The resistance put up by the Jews and bandits could only be suppressed by energetic actions of our troops day and night. The Reichsfuehrer SS ordered, therefore, on 4/23/1943, the cleaning out of the ghetto with utter ruthlessness and merciless tenacity. I, therefore, decided to destroy and burn down the entire ghetto without regard to the armament factories. These factories were systematically dismantled and then burned. Jews usually left their hideouts, but frequently remained in the burning buildings and jumped out of the windows only when the heat became unbearable. They then tried to crawl with broken bones across the street into buildings which were not afire. Sometimes they changed their hideouts during the night into the ruins of burned buildings. Life in the sewers was not pleasant after the first week. Many times we could hear loud voices in the sewers. SS men or policemen climbed bravely through the manholes to capture these Jews. Sometimes they stumbled over Jewish corpses: sometimes they were shot at. Tear gas bombs were thrown

into the manholes and the Jews driven out of the sewers and captured. Countless numbers of Jews were liquidated in sewers and bunkers through blasting. The longer the resistance continued the tougher became the members of the Waffen SS, Police and Wehrmacht who always discharged their duties in an exemplary manner. Frequently Jews who tried to replenish their food supplies during the night or to communicate with neighboring groups were exterminated.

"This action eliminated," says the SS commander, "a proved total of 56,065. To that, we have to add the number killed through blasting, fire, etc., which cannot be counted."

We charge that all atrocities against Jews were the manifestation and culmination of the Nazi plan to which every defendant here was a party. I know very well that some of these men did take steps to spare some particular Jew for some personal reason from the horrors that awaited the unrescued Jew. Some protested that particular atrocities were excessive, and discredited the general policy. While a few defendants may show efforts to make specific exceptions to the policy of Jewish extermination, I have found no instance in which any defendant opposed the policy itself or sought to revoke or even modify it. . . .

Mystery and suspense was added to cruelty in order to spread torture from the inmate to his family and friends. Men and women disappeared from their homes or business or from the streets and no word came of them. The omission of notice was not due to overworked staff; it was due to policy. The Chief of the SD and SIPO reported that in accordance with orders from the Fuehrer anxiety should be created in the minds of the family of the arrested person. . . .

To clumsy cruelty, scientific skill was added. "Undesirables" were exterminated by injection of drugs into the bloodstream, by asphyxiation in gas chambers. They were shot with poison bullets, to study the effects.

Then, to cruel experiments the Nazis added obscene ones. These were not the work of underling-degenerates but of master-minds high in the Nazi conspiracy. On 5/20/1942 General Field Marshal Milch authorized SS General Wolff to go ahead at Dachau Camp with so-called "cold experiments"; and four female gypsies were supplied for the purpose. Himmler gave permission to carry on these "experiments" also in other camps. At Dachau, the reports of the "doctor" in charge show that victims immersed in cold water until their body temperature was reduced to 28C (82.4 degrees Fahrenheit), when they died immediately. This was in 8/1942. But the "doctor's" technique improved. By 2/1943 he was able to report that 30 persons were chilled to 27–29 degrees, their hands and feet frozen white, and their bodies "rewarmed" by a hot bath. But the Nazi scientific triumph was "rewarming with animal heat." The victim, all but frozen to death, was surrounded with bodies of living women until he revived and responded to his environment by having sexual intercourse. Here Nazi degeneracy reached its nadir. . . .

War of Aggression

I will not prolong this address by detailing the steps leading to the war of aggression which began with the invasion of Poland on 9/1/1939. The further story will be unfolded to you from documents including those of the German High Command itself. . . .

As early as 11/5/1937 Hitler told Defendants Goering, Raeder, and Neurath, among others, that German rearmament was practically accomplished and that he had decided to secure by force, starting with a lightning attack [on] Czechoslovakia and Austria, greater living space for German Europe no later than 1943–1945 and perhaps as early as 1938. . . .

On 8/22/1939 Hitler again addressed members of the High Command, telling them when the start of military operations would be ordered. He disclosed that for propaganda purposes, he would provocate a good reason. "It will make no difference," he announced, "whether this reason will sound convincing or not. After all, the victor will not be asked whether he talked the truth or not. We have to proceed brutally. The stronger is always right." On 11/23/1939, after the Germans had invaded Poland, Hitler made this explanation:

> . . . For the first time in history we have to fight on only one front, the other front is at present free. But no one can know how long that will remain so. I have doubted for a long time whether I should strike in the East and then in the West. Basically I did not organize the armed forces in order not to strike. The decision

to strike was always in me. Earlier or later I wanted to solve the problem. Under pressure it was decided that the East was to be attacked first. . . .

We know the bloody sequel. Frontier incidents were staged. Demands were made for cession of territory. When Poland refused, the German forces invaded on 9/1/1939. Warsaw was destroyed; Poland fell. The Nazis, in accordance with plan, moved swiftly to extend their aggression throughout Europe and to gain the advantage of surprise over their unprepared neighbors. Despite repeated and solemn assurances of peaceful intentions, they invaded Denmark and Norway on 4/9/1940; Belgium, The Netherlands and Luxembourg on 5/10/1940; Yugoslavia and Greece on 4/6/1941.

As part of the Nazi preparation for aggression against Poland and her allies, Germany, on 8/23/1939, had entered into a non-aggression pact with Soviet Russia. It was only a delaying treaty intended to be kept no longer than necessary to prepare for its violation. On 6/22/1941, pursuant to long-matured plans, the Nazis hurled troops into Soviet territory without any declaration of war. The entire European world was aflame.

Conspiracy with Japan

The Nazi plans of aggression called for use of Asiatic allies and they found among the Japanese men of kindred mind and purpose. . . .

On 9/27/1940 the Nazis concluded a German-Italian-Japanese 10-year military and economic alliance by which those powers agreed "to stand by and cooperate with one another in regard to their efforts in Greater East Asia and regions of Europe respectively wherein it is their prime purpose to establish and maintain a new order of things."

On 3/5/1941 a top-secret directive was issued by Defendant Keitel. It stated that the Fuehrer had ordered instigation of Japan's active participation in the war and directed that Japan's military power has to be strengthened by the disclosure of German war experiences and support of a military, economic, and technical nature has to be given. The aim was stated to be to crush England quickly thereby keeping the United States out of the war. . . .

The proofs in this case will also show that the leaders of

Germany were planning war against the United States from its Atlantic as well as instigating it from its Pacific approaches. A captured memorandum from the Fuehrer's headquarters, dated 10/29/1940, asks certain information as to air bases and supplies and reports further that: "The Fuehrer is at present occupied with the question of the occupation of the Atlantic islands with a view to the prosecution of war against America at a later date. Deliberations on this subject are being embarked upon here.". . .

Crimes in the Conduct of War

Even the most warlike of peoples have recognized in the name of humanity some limitations on the savagery of warfare. Rules to that end have been embodied in international conventions to which Germany became a party. This code had prescribed certain restraints as to the treatment of belligerents. The enemy was entitled to surrender and to receive quarter and good treatment as a prisoner of war. We will show by German documents that these rights were denied, that prisoners of war were given brutal treatment and often murdered. . . .

It was ordered that captured English and American airmen should no longer be granted the status of prisoners of war. They were to be treated as criminals and the Army was ordered to refrain from protecting them against lynching by the populace. The Nazi Government, through its police and propaganda agencies, took pains to incite the civilian population to attack and kill airmen who crash-landed. . . .

Only remnants of the European Jewish population remain in Germany.

Similarly, we will show Hitler's top secret order, dated 10/18/1942, that commandos, regardless of condition, were "to be slaughtered to the last man" after capture. We will [show] how the circulation of secret orders, one of which was signed by Hess, to be passed orally to civilians, that enemy fliers or parachutists were to be arrested or liquidated. By such means were murders incited and directed. . . .

The Nazi purpose was to leave Germany's neighbors so weakened that even if she should eventually lose the war, she would still be the most powerful nation in Europe. Against this background, we must view the plan for ruthless warfare, which means a plan for the commission of War Crimes and Crimes against Humanity.

Hostages in large numbers were demanded and killed. Mass punishments were inflicted, so savage that whole communities were extinguished. . . .

Slave Labor and Looting

Perhaps the deportation to slave labor was the most horrible and extensive slaving operation in history. On few other subjects is our evidence so abundant or so damaging. In a speech made on 1/25/1944 the Defendant Frank, Governor General of Poland, boasted, "I have sent 1.3 million Polish workers into the Reich." The Defendant Sauckel reported that "out of the 5 million foreign workers who arrived in Germany not even 200,000 came voluntarily.". . .

Not only was there a purpose to debilitate and demoralize the economy of Germany's neighbors for the purpose of destroying their competitive position, but there was looting and pilfering on an unprecedented scale. We need not be hypocritical about this business of looting. I recognize that no army moves through occupied territory without some pilfering as it goes. Usually the amount of pilfering increases as discipline wanes. If the evidence in this case showed no looting except of that sort, I certainly would ask no conviction of these defendants for it.

But we will show you that looting was not due to the lack of discipline or to the ordinary weaknesses of human nature. The German organized plundering, planned it, disciplined it, and made it official just as he organized everything else, and then he compiled the most meticulous records to show that he had done the best job of looting that was possible under the circumstances. And we have those records.

The Defendant Rosenberg was put in charge of a systematic plundering of the art objects of Europe by direct order of Hitler dated 1/29/1940. On 4/16/1943 Rosenberg reported that up to the 7th of April, 92 railway cars with 2775 cases containing art objects had been sent to Germany; and that 53 pieces of art had been shipped to Hitler direct, and 594 to the Defendant Goering. The report mentioned something like 20,000 pieces of seized art and the main locations where they were stored.

Moreover this looting was glorified by Rosenberg. Here we have 39 leather-bound tabulated volumes of his inventory, which in due time we will offer in evidence. One cannot but admire the artistry of this Rosenberg report. The Nazi taste was cosmopolitan. Of the 9455 articles inventoried, there were included 5255 paintings, 297 sculptures, 1372 pieces of antique furniture, 307 textiles, and 2224 small objects of art. Rosenberg observed that there were approximately 10,000 more objects still to be inventoried. Rosenberg himself estimated that the values involved would cone close to a billion dollars. . . .

The Law

Of course, it was, under the law of all civilized peoples, a crime for one man with his bare knuckles to assault another. How did it come that multiplying this crime by a million, and adding fire arms to bare knuckles, made it a legally innocent act? The doctrine was that one could not be regarded as criminal for committing the usual violent acts in the conduct of legitimate warfare. The age of imperialistic expansion during the eighteenth and nineteenth centuries added the foul doctrine, contrary to the teachings of early Christian and international law scholars such as Grotius, that all wars are to be regarded as legitimate wars. The sum of these two doctrines was to give war-making a complete immunity from accountability to law.

This was intolerable for an age that called itself civilized. Plain people with their earthy common sense, revolted at such fictions and legalisms so contrary to ethical principles and demanded checks on war immunities. Statesmen and international lawyers at first cautiously responded by adopting rules of warfare designed to make the conduct of war more civilized. The effort was to set legal limits to the violence that could be done to civilian populations and to combatants as well.

The common sense of men after the first World War demanded, however, that the law's condemnation of war reach deeper, and that the law condemn not merely uncivilized ways of waging war, but also the waging in any way of uncivilized wars—wars of aggression. The world's statesmen again went only as far as they were forced to go. Their efforts were timid and cautious and often less explicit than we might have hoped. But the 1920s did outlaw aggressive war.

The re-establishment of the principle that there are unjust wars and that unjust wars are illegal is traceable in many steps. One of the most significant is the Briand-Kellogg Pact of 1928, by which Germany, Italy, and Japan, in common with practically all nations of the world, renounced war as an instrument of national policy, bound themselves to seek the settlement of disputes only by pacific means, and condemned recourse to war for the solution of international controversies. . . .

We charge that all atrocities against Jews were the manifestation and culmination of the Nazi plan.

Any resort to war—to any kind of a war—is a resort to means that are inherently criminal. War inevitably is a course of killings, assaults, deprivations of liberty, and destruction of property. An honestly defensive war is, of course, legal and saves those lawfully conducting it from criminality. But inherently criminal acts cannot be defended by showing that those who committed them were engaged in a war, when war itself is illegal. The very minimum legal consequence of the treaties making aggressive wars illegal is to strip those who incite or wage them of every defense the law ever gave, and to leave war-makers subject to judgment by the usually accepted principles of the law of crimes.

But if it be thought that the Charter, whose declarations concededly bind us all, does contain new law I still do not shrink from demanding its strict application by this Tribunal. The rule of law in the world, flouted by the lawlessness incited by these defendants, had to be restored at the cost to my country of over a million casualties, not to mention those of other nations. I cannot subscribe to the perverted reasoning that society may advance and strengthen the rule of law by the expenditure of morally innocent lives but that progress in the law may never be made at the price of morally guilty lives. . . .

The Crime Against Peace

A basic provision of the Charter is that to plan, prepare, initiate, or wage a war of aggression, or a war in violation of international treaties, agreements, and assurances, or to conspire or participate in a common plan to do so, is a crime.

It is perhaps a weakness in this Charter that it fails itself to define a war of aggression. . . .

I suggest that an "aggressor" is generally held to be that state which is the first to commit any of the following actions:

(1) Declaration of war upon another state;

(2) Invasion by its armed forces, with or without a declaration of war, of the territory of another state;

(3) Attack by its land, naval, or air forces, with or without a declaration of war, on the territory, vessels or aircraft of another state; and

(4) Provision of support to armed bands formed in the territory of another state, or refusal, notwithstanding the request of the invaded state, to take in its own territory, all the measures in its power to deprive those bands of all assistance or protection.

And I further suggest that it is the general view that no political, military, economic, or other considerations shall serve as an excuse or justification for such actions; but exercise of the right of legitimate self-defense, that is to say, resistance to an act of aggression, or action to assist a state which has been subjected to aggression, shall not constitute a war of aggression.

It is upon such an understanding of the law that our evidence of a conspiracy to provoke and wage an aggressive war is prepared and presented. By this test each of the series of wars begun by these Nazi leaders was unambiguously aggressive. . . .

Our position is that whatever grievances a nation may have, however objectionable it finds the status quo, aggressive warfare is illegal means for settling those grievances or for altering those conditions. It may be that the Germany of the 1920s and 1930s faced desperate problems, problems that would have warranted the boldest measures short of war. All other methods—persuasion, propaganda, economic competition, diplomacy—were open to an aggrieved country, but aggressive warfare was outlawed. These defendants did make aggressive war, a war in violation of treaties. They did attack and invade their neighbors in order to effectuate a foreign policy which they knew could not be accomplished by measures short of war. And that is as far as we accuse or propose to inquire. . . .

The Charter recognizes that one who has committed

criminal acts may not take refuge in superior orders nor in the doctrine that his crimes were acts of states. These twin principles working together have heretofore resulted in immunity for practically everyone concerned in the really great crimes against peace and mankind. Those in lower ranks were protected against liability by the orders of their superiors. The superiors were protected because their orders were called acts of state. Under the Charter, no defense based on either of these doctrines can be entertained. Modern civilization puts unlimited weapons of destruction in the hands of men. It cannot tolerate so vast an area of legal irresponsibility. Even the German Military Code provides that: "If the execution of a military order in the course of duty violates the criminal law, then the superior officer giving the order will bear the sole responsibility therefor. However, the obeying subordinate will share the punishment of the participant: (1) if he has exceeded the order given to him, or (2) if it was within his knowledge that the order of his superior officer concerned an act by which it was intended to commit a civil or military crime or transgression." Of course, we do not argue that the circumstances under which one commits an act should be disregarded in judging its legal effect. A conscripted private on a firing squad cannot expect to hold an inquest on the validity of the execution. The Charter implies common sense limits to liability just as it places common sense limits upon immunity. But none of these men before you acted in minor parts. Each of them was entrusted with broad discretion and exercised great power. Their responsibility is correspondingly great and may not be shifted to that fictional being, "the State," which cannot be produced for trial, cannot testify, and cannot be sentenced.

The Nazi government . . . took pains to incite the civilian population to attack and kill airmen who crash-landed.

The Charter also recognizes a vicarious liability, which responsibility recognized by most modern systems of law, for acts committed by others in carrying out a common plan or conspiracy to which a defendant has become a party. I need not discuss the familiar principles of such liability. Every day in the courts of countries associated in this prosecution, men are convicted for acts that they did not personally commit, but for which they were held responsible because of membership in illegal combinations or plans or conspiracies. . . .

The Trial's Goals

I am too well aware of the weaknesses of juridical action alone to contend that in itself your decision under this Charter can prevent future wars. Judicial action always comes after the event. Wars are started only on the theory and in the confidence that they can be won. Personal punishment, to be suffered only in the event the war is lost, will probably not be a sufficient deterrent to prevent a war where the warmakers feel the chances of defeat to be negligible.

But the ultimate step in avoiding periodic wars, which are inevitable in a system of international lawlessness, is to make statesmen responsible to law. And let me make clear that while this law is first applied against German aggressors, the law includes, and if it is to serve a useful purpose it must condemn aggression by any other nations, including those which sit here now in judgment. We are able to do away with domestic tyranny and violence and aggression by those in power against the rights of their own people only when we make all men answerable to the law. This trial represents mankind's desperate effort to apply the discipline of the law to statesmen who have used their powers of state to attack the foundations of the world's peace and to commit aggressions against the rights of their neighbors. . . .

Civilization asks whether law is so laggard as to be utterly helpless to deal with crimes of this magnitude by criminals of this order of importance. It does not expect that you can make war impossible. It does expect that your juridical action will put the forces of international law, its precepts, its prohibitions and, most of all, its sanctions, on the side of peace, so that men and women of good will, in all countries, may have "leave to live by no man's leave, underneath the law."

Chapter **2**

Was the Nuremberg Trial Just?

1

A Just Trial

Charles E. Wyzanski Jr.

At the time of the trial, Charles E. Wyzanski Jr. wrote a cautionary article anticipating that the rights of the accused would be trampled and a bad precedent would be set for the future. After the trial, he admitted that he had been wrong. In particular, he concluded that failing to create a new legal standard that ensured the Nazis would be prosecuted could have opened the door to more arbitrary punishments. Even though the judge was reassured after seeing how the trial was conducted, he still believed it could have been done more fairly by, for example, including neutral parties in the proceedings—though he admits the Russians probably would not have allowed this. Wyzanski also came to appreciate some of the positive aspects of the trial, such as the acquisition of documentary evidence that might have otherwise not been discovered or publicly disclosed. Charles E. Wyzanski Jr. was a judge of the U.S. District Court for Massachusetts.

The doubt which seemed to critics of the Nuremberg trial most fundamental was whether the defendants could properly be held to answer a charge that they had engaged in "the crime of aggressive war." Was there any such substantive offense?

Many who replied affirmatively contended that "the crime of aggressive war" was no different from the specific war crimes (such as killing a captured enemy civilian) that had been defined in the Hague Convention of 1907. That is, they argued that waging an aggressive war was a crime that had been outlawed by a specific treaty or treaties; and

From "Nuremberg in Retrospect," by Charles E. Wyzanski Jr., *The Atlantic Monthly*, December 1946.

that individuals who engaged in such conduct, like individuals who engaged in the slaughter of captured civilians, were triable by any tribunal established for the occasion by a warring power, and were punishable by any penalty prescribed for the occasion by that power.

That argument seems to me unsound. It does not seem to me that an examination of the pre-war treaties, conference proposals, diplomatic correspondence, and juristic writings shows that there was a specific international covenant that individuals who waged an aggressive war were criminals in the same sense that there was a specific international covenant that individuals who killed captured civilians were criminals.

But it is not sufficient to stop with that purely analytical approach. There remains this inquiry: Is it just to declare, after hostilities have begun, that planners of an aggressive war are criminals?

Those who believe that it is, make a twofold contention. First, they say that when these defendants planned this war both they and everyone else would have admitted that the planning of aggressive war was a violation of standards which, whether or not they had been formulated like the Hague conventions, were universally accepted by the international community in treaties and otherwise; and that no one should be surprised to see such deliberate violations stamped as criminal. Second, they say that international criminal law in its present almost primitive state is similar to early domestic criminal law, and therefore requires not only the application of enacted law and of judicial precedent, but also the retroactive declaration of new law.

At first I was shocked by those contentions. I was prepared to assent to the statement that the defendants deliberately violated standards which had been widely accepted. But I hesitated to concede that any state or group of states should have the power retroactively to affix the additional label "criminal" to conduct which, when it occurred, was commonly regarded only as a violation of accepted standards and of treaties. It seemed to me that to allow such retrospective labeling opened the door to an arbitrary selection of offenders. It struck at the roots of constitutional limitations on power and contradicted the teachings of the philosophers of liberty. Moreover, while I was prepared to assent to the proposition that some topics in international law could be, and had been, developed by judicial tribunals declaring the law retroactively, I was not aware that the particular branch of international law which dealt with individual crimes had ever been thought to be susceptible of retroactive codification by judges or by states.

Lesser Evil

On further reflection I have come to the view that the points stated in the last paragraph are not conclusive. I am now persuaded that in the formative period of international law it is just for a representative group of power retroactively to label as criminal, conduct which, when it occurred, was universally regarded as a serious violation of generally accepted international standards and treaties. To put it in a single sentence, the reasons for my change are that the failure of the international community to attach the criminal label to such universally condemned conduct would be more likely to promote arbitrary and discriminatory action by public authorities and to undermine confidence in the proposition that international agreements are made to be kept, than the failure of the international community to abide by the maxim that no act can be punished as a crime unless there was in advance of the act a specific criminal law.

It is a choice of evil. And I do not claim that my present belief can be proved to be correct. Essentially it is what the philosophers would call a value judgment based on these considerations. If the powers had not agreed upon a rational formula for indicting those who planned World War II, it is highly probable that either some state or some unauthorized individuals would arbitrarily and perhaps even ruthlessly have undertaken the punishment of capriciously chosen Nazi chieftains. If the treaties against aggression which had been negotiated prior to World War II were treated as mere statements of intention, then post-war treaties against aggression, no matter how precisely drafted, would have been regarded as imperfect obligations.

But, regardless of its provability, the scale of values which now seems to me sound puts repugnance to retroactive legislation in a less important place than repugnance to leaving unpunished serious violations of standards universally recognized by the international community and embodied in treaties and like international obligations. To guard against misapprehension, I should reiterate that the scale applies only to grave departures from standards that have been widely and formally accepted, and only when the conduct arises in the international field where and while the organs of the international community are so undeveloped and are so intermittent in their functioning that it is impractical to expect the declaration of criminality to be made in advance of the conduct.

Thus it now seems to me to have been "just," and even probably under some civilized systems of law even "legal," to have charged the defendants with the crime of aggressive war. But, in candor, I must add that I am not satisfied that it was "legal" under American law. I can best express my reservation by example. Suppose that Hess had been brought to the United States and had been here charged with, tried on, and convicted of only the crime of aggressive war by a military tribunal created by the President with or without the cooperation of other nations; and suppose that, having been sentenced to jail in the United States, he, like Yamashita, had sought a writ of habeas corpus from a United States judge. Would he not have had a right to be released on the ground that he was held in violation of the ex post facto clause of Article I, Section 9, of the United States Constitution? That is, does not the United States Constitution put at the very front of its scale of values a ban on retroactive criminal laws?

It now seems to me to have been "just"... to have charged the defendants with the crime of aggressive war.

Before turning to the next topic, I should note parenthetically that some persons who shared my original view, that before the Nuremberg trial there was no substantive "crime of aggressive war," say that even after the Nuremberg trial they do not know what the crime is, because the victorious powers and their court have not defined the crime of which the defendants were adjudged guilty. To them the verdict implies no more than the proposition that the victors are empowered to punish the vanquished. They say that there is no definition as to when a war is "aggressive" and that there is no rule laid down for distinguishing between the organizers and the participants in such an aggressive war.

To this the answers are that the definition of "aggressive," like other legal terms, will acquire content by exemplification; and the full meaning will become clear only after sufficient cases have been brought before and adjudicated by competent tribunals. It may be difficult at some future time to determine whether a particular war is an aggressive war, but there was no difficulty in deciding that the Nazi war was an aggressive war, since it would be generally conceded that the term "aggressive war" at its least includes a war like the Nazi war, which is begun by an attack by those who do not themselves believe that they are in danger of immediate attack by others. And although it may be difficult to say how far down the line of command responsibility goes, responsibility certainly extends at least to those who, knowing there is no danger, both plan and direct the unwarranted attack.

These answers would have been more evident if it had not been for the almost absurd citations of Hugo Grotius and other jurists made by some supporters of the Nuremberg proceedings. These supporters often seem to argue that Grotius said (which, of course, he did not) that those who kill in the course of a war commit a legal crime unless the war is a just war; and that where a war is unjust, those who engage in it and kill their fellow men are murderers. Grotius's definitions of just and unjust wars refer primarily not to mundane but to divine justice. And he did not describe—few sensible people would describe—as murderer the common soldier required to kill his enemy in the course of an unjust war. Neither Grotius nor the powers who drafted the Nuremberg charter nor the judges or prosecutors who participated at Nuremberg have termed criminal those men who merely fought in a war not of their making. . . .

Judging the Judges

While, so far as I am aware, it was legally unobjectionable to have the defendants tried by an English judge or a French judge or an American judge, or any combination of them, can we fairly say it was unobjectionable to have the defendants tried by a Russian judge on the particular charge of aggressive war which was presented? Did not the charge refer to an aggressive attack on Poland? And (while deeply

sensible of the later horrible sufferings the Russians under-
went from an unprovoked attack by Germany on Russia itself) can we say that the Russians (who in advance were ap-
prised of the proposed German attack on Poland and who
participated in the division of the spoils resulting from that
attack) were suitable persons to participate in judgment
upon the charge that the Germans aggressively attacked
Poland? This is not an issue (as it is sometimes supposed to
be) whether it is just to prosecute one group of criminals
(Germans) and not another (Russians). It is the simpler issue whether an apparent confederate is to sit in judgment
on an alleged criminal.

While it was not legally necessary to have invited neutrals and even distinguished anti-Nazi Germans to sit in
judgment at the trial, would it not have been politically
wiser to have done so, since the type of issues raised by a
charge of the crime of aggressive war, unlike the issues
raised by a charge of strict war crimes, are so susceptible of
national bias? Would not a tribunal which included some
judges free of any connection with the victims of the aggressive attack have furnished a sounder precedent?

To these questions the usual, but not entirely satisfactory, answers are that the authors of the Nuremberg procedure believed that distinguished neutrals would not accept appointment, and that the Russians would not have sat
with neutrals.

Two other political, rather than legal, questions remain.
First, was it desirable to include this charge in the Nuremberg indictment when there were enough other charges of
a more orthodox character upon which the defendants were
being tried and were likely to be hanged? Second, was it
better to have these defendants tried before a military court
or to have them disposed of by a more summary executive
procedure?

The Aggressive War Charge

If the defendants had been tried solely on the grounds that
they had engaged in war crimes in the strict sense and in
crimes against humanity, the practical result for the men in
the dock at Nuremberg would (with the single exception of
Hess) have been precisely the same as it actually turned out
to be. Hess is the only defendant who was convicted of the
crime of aggressive war and the crime of conspiracy but was

not convicted of other crimes as well.

Moreover, if the defendants had been tried solely on the grounds that they had engaged in war crimes in the strict sense and in crimes against humanity, there would from the outset have been a far greater degree of unanimity of professional opinion in support of the Nuremberg trial.

There were, however, countervailing considerations, which could well be thought more significant. If the defendants were charged only with the strict war crimes and not with the crime of aggressive war, it would have deeply offended the public sense of justice, for the public regarded the planning of the war as the greatest of crimes. To the general public it would have seemed grossly inappropriate to punish Goring only for killing a few named individuals, and not for starting a war in which millions were killed.

Furthermore, if the powers had not included in the Nuremberg indictment a charge that the defendants had committed the crime of aggressive war, not only would they have missed the opportunity to establish the doctrine that there is a world law against aggressive war, but their very silence and timidity would have weakened the force now, and perhaps for all time, of such declarations as had heretofore been made that aggressive war was outlawed.

Judicial vs. Executive Proceeding

There remains for discussion the problem whether it would have been politically wiser to have dealt with the Nuremberg defendants by a proceeding that was not judicial but frankly executive.

Before the Nuremberg trial began, those who, like myself, originally opposed a judicial proceeding stressed the following points, among others. There was a grave danger that the trial itself could not be conducted in an orderly way. . . . There seemed no likelihood that the trial would be so arranged that the defendants would be given adequate opportunity to produce evidence and to examine and cross-examine witnesses. There was skepticism as to whether any defendant had a chance to be acquitted, particularly since it appeared that the tribunal might start with a presumption of guilt rather than a presumption of innocence. And it was feared that the tribunal would focus on the propaganda aspects of the trial and would be unduly concerned with the effect of the trial upon the public opinion of the outside world. Cumulatively, these considerations made many commentators doubtful whether the court could act as a court should act. And—though this was less important—it made commentators fear that the trial instead of persuading the Germans of today or tomorrow that our side was just, would persuade them that we were hypocrites disguising vengeance under the facade of legality.

Judged as a court trial, the Nuremberg
proceedings were a model of forensic fairness.

To avoid such dangers, these critics suggested that victorious powers should frankly state that for reasons which would be announced to the world, and which would include a recital of the wrongs the defendants had perpetrated and the menace they still presented, the powers proposed to deny them further liberty and, if necessary, to take their lives. Before such announcement was put into effect, the persons named for punishment would have an adequate opportunity to present any evidence they had that they had been erroneously named or charged with wrongdoing. It was believed that a course so drastic and so plainly premised on an exceptional situation would never be thought, as a trial might be thought, suitable for incorporation in the permanent fabric of domestic systems of justice.

Now that the trial has been held, many of these forebodings are shown to have been wide of the mark. Judged as a court trial, the Nuremberg proceedings were a model of forensic fairness. Lord Justice Lawrence and his associates acted with dignity and firmness and with eyes directed only to such matters as judges ought to consider.

Moreover, the very length of the trial has shown that those who originally favored a summary proceeding had overestimated the knowledge which the Allies had in advance of the trial. A year ago they did not have the specific information necessary promptly to prepare a reliable recital of who were the chief offenders and what were their offenses. Indeed, if it had not been for the trial and the diligent efforts of the staff of able lawyers and investigators, acting promptly and in response to the necessities of legal technique, the important documents in which the defendants convicted themselves might never have been uncovered. Thus the trial gave the victorious powers the adequate record which they required for proper disposition of the defendants and simultaneously gave historians much of the data which the world will require for proper evaluation of the causes and events of World War II.

But the outstanding accomplishment of the trial which could never have been achieved by any more summary executive action, is that it has crystallized the concept that there already is inherent in the international community a machinery both for the expression of international criminal law and for its enforcement. The great powers of the world have agreed that it is in accordance with justice for a group of nations to establish on an ad hoc basis a tribunal, first, to review the state of world opinion on conduct, in order to determine whether that conduct, when it occurred, was so universally condemned as an international wrong that it can be called a "crime"; and second, to apply that determination to individuals.

No doubt such an ad hoc method is not satisfactory as a covenant made by all the powers in advance of wrongful conduct—a covenant describing such conduct, fixing the tribunal which shall try offenders and fixing the penalty which shall be imposed. But until the world is prepared to follow the more satisfactory method, it has every reason to be profoundly grateful to Mr. Justice Jackson and his associates, who, in the face of enormous practical difficulties and widespread theoretical criticisms, persisted until they demonstrated the justice of the ad hoc method adopted at Nuremberg.

2

Victors' Justice?

Michael Biddiss

The Nuremberg Trial differed from conventional trials in numerous ways. Legal procedures were different, the standards applied were a mixture of various traditions, and many of the decisions about the trial's conduct were more political than legal. Another distinction was the motivation behind the trial. One principal motivation was to mete out justice, which the Allies agreed in advance meant punishment for crimes the Nazis committed. Another purpose was educational; that is, to expose the full range of Germany's illegal activities. The long-range intent of the trial was to establish a standard for international conduct and send a message to those who might contemplate aggression in the future. The goals were noble, but the question arose as to whether the Allies could pursue them fairly. As victors in the war, they were making the rules by which the Nazis were to be judged and holding the Germans alone responsible for crimes committed during the war while evading any responsibility for their own misdeeds. In this excerpt, Michael Biddiss discusses some of the contentious issues that arose in preparing for the trial and the failure of the tribunal to achieve all of its objectives. Biddiss is a history professor at the University of Reading.

Fifty years on, the Nuremberg Trial continues to haunt us. This is not simply a matter of the Nazi horrors revealed or confirmed in the courtroom. It is a question also of the weaknesses and strengths of the proceedings themselves. The undoubted flaws rightly continue to trouble the thoughtful. Yet, equally, we remain disturbed by the fact that, over the subsequent half-century, the world community has done so little to build upon the positive features also attaching to this great event.

The enormity of the murderous terror unleashed by the Third Reich is now so evident to us that the mounting of some full-scale trial of its defeated leaders might well seem, in retrospect, entirely inevitable. The path to Nuremberg was, however, much more tortuous than that. The Moscow Declaration of November 1943 certainly made plain the aim of Roosevelt, Stalin and Churchill to punish, by some form of joint action, those major Nazis whose offences could not be regarded as limited to any particular geographical location. Yet, as Germany's defeat approached, there was urgent need for the Allies to become less vague about actual procedures.

During the Tehran Conference at the end of 1943, Stalin had toasted the justice of the firing squad and mentioned the need for 50,000 shootings. Roosevelt and Churchill seem to have been shocked by the number, even while sympathising with the method. In any case, the Soviet leader was probably jesting—something suggested by the fact that his regime (itself well-versed in the propagandist value of political trials) remained thereafter consistent in its demand for some form of detailed judicial enquiry. Conversely, it was the American and British governments that continued in 1944 to focus chiefly on schemes of summary process and prompt execution. Not until early 1945 did Roosevelt become fully converted to the 'Bernays Plan,' devised during the previous September within the US Department of War. Once this proposal concerning comprehensive legal proceedings had won the day in Washington, Churchill found himself facing combined American and Soviet pressure to mount a major trial conducted by some specially constituted international tribunal.

In London there was particularly stout resistance from the head of the judiciary, Lord Chancellor Simon. He stood by the advice which he had previously given to the Cabinet:

> I am strongly of the opinion that the method by trial, conviction, and judicial sentence is quite inappropriate for notorious ringleaders such as Hitler, Himmler, Goering, Goebbels, and Ribbentrop. Apart from the formidable difficulties of constituting the Court, for-

mulating the charge, and assembling the evidence, the question of their fate is a political, not a judicial, question. It could not rest with judges, however eminent or learned, to decide finally a matter like this, which is of the widest and most vital public policy.

There was some justification for Simon's anxiety about unavoidably protracted proceedings. He was deeply concerned lest an international public should come to see them simply as a 'put-up job' designed by the Allies to validate a series of prejudged punishments. Were the precedents for this kind of trial so weak as to prompt the condemnation that it amounted to nothing more than 'victors' justice'? And was there not great danger that, at certain points in such a process, Hitler and his colleagues might manage to reverse the arguments so as to embarrass the Allied case?

Whom to Try

Only in May 1945—by which time the Fuhrer himself was dead, and victory in Europe had been assured—did the British government finally yield to the American and Soviet policy of full-scale trial. Under the new Truman presidency a US delegation, headed by Justice Jackson of the Supreme Court, was principally responsible for driving the project forward in such a way that by August 8th (ironically, the same week as the Hiroshima and Nagasaki bombings), a series of ground-rules had been settled through the so-called London Agreement. With France now included among the signatories, the resulting Charter created a four-power International Military Tribunal. To this each government would appoint one judge plus a deputy, as well as supplying the court with prosecuting staff. The members of the Tribunal soon chose the senior British nominee, Lord Justice Geoffrey Lawrence, to preside over hearings that eventually stretched from November 1945 to October 1946. His alternate, Sir Norman Birkett, was surely right to believe that they were embarking on 'the greatest trial in history.'

Meanwhile, the Allies had been debating the roster of potential defendants. Hitler, Himmler, Goebbels and Heydrich were the principal figures who had not survived even to be indicted. As for Bormann, he could not be found either alive or dead, and thus was tried in absence. Any critical reading of the trial transcripts has to take account of the tendency for most of the other twenty-one defendants (see table), all of whom did appear in the Palace of Justice at Nuremberg assisted by their own defence counsel, to shift responsibility for wrongdoing towards those leading Nazis who were not present. The accused had been chosen largely to ensure representation of all the major administrative

Defendants, Charges, Verdicts and Sentences

This listing of defendants follows the order of the indictment.
G = Guilty; NG = Not Guilty

Defendant	Count 1	Count 2	Count 3	Count 4	Sentence
Hermann Goring	G	G	G	G	Hanging
Rudolf Hess	G	G	NG	NG	Life
Joachim von Ribbentrop	G	G	G	G	Hanging
Wilhelm Keitel	G	G	G	G	Hanging
Ernst Kaltenbrunner	NG		G	G	Hanging
Alfred Rosenberg	G	G	G	G	Hanging
Hans Frank	NG		G	G	Hanging
Wilhelm Frick	NG	G	G	G	Hanging
Julius Streicher	NG			G	Hanging
Walther Funk	NG	G	G	G	Life
Hjalmar Schacht	NG	NG			Acquitted
Karl Donitz	NG	G	G		10 Years
Erich Raeder	G	G	G		Life
Baldur von Schirach	NG			G	20 Years
Fritz Sauckel	NG	NG	G	G	Hanging
Alfred Jodl	G	G	G	G	Hanging
Martin Bormann (absent)	NG		G	G	Hanging
Franz von Papen	NG	NG			Acquitted
Arthur Seyss-Inquart	NG	G	G	G	Hanging
Albert Speer	NG	NG	G	G	20 Years
Constantin von Neurath	G	G	G	G	15 Years
Hans Fritzsche	NG		NG	NG	Acquitted
Total Guilty	8	12	16	16	
Not Guilty	14	4	2	2	

groupings within the Reich, and thus to reflect the American emphasis on establishing the criminality of these organisations through judgements that could be treated as immune from further challenge during later denazification proceedings. Yet, perhaps inevitably, lawyers and public alike came to focus mainly on the human dimension to Nuremberg, as a trial of humiliated Nazi bosses (including the closest surviving associates of the Fuhrer) and as a record of their victims' suffering.

The Allies could have got most of what they wanted . . . by limiting their prosecution solely to "war crimes" and "crimes against humanity."

The prisoners themselves were not readily reducible to any single stereotype of Fascist leadership. In the case of Ernst Kaltenbrunner, latterly Chief of the Security Service, and of Hans Frank, the butchering Governor-General of occupied Poland, a stark brutality was plain. This also characterised the virulently anti-Semitic Julius Streicher, but here—as with Hitler's former deputy, Rudolf Hess—queries about insanity too were at issue. Seeking to maintain a certain distance from all these were four senior officers, Alfred Jodl and Wilhelm Keitel of the army, together with Eric Raeder and Karl Donitz from the navy. This quartet centred its defence on necessities of military obedience which the Allies were deemed incompetent to challenge. Similar indignation at the impropriety of summons before the Tribunal marked the hearing of the old conservatives, Franz von Papen and Constantin von Neurath, as well as that of Hjalmar Schacht, the banker who had helped to put Hitler's Reich on the road to economic recovery. As the trial proceeded, certain other defendants became increasingly revealed as over-promoted mediocrities: among them were Joachim von Ribbentrop of the Foreign Office, the self-styled 'philosopher' Alfred Rosenberg who had enjoyed formal responsibility for the Eastern Occupied Territories, and the painfully inarticulate Fritz Sauckel who had run the programme of slave labour.

These same helot battalions had been most directly exploited by Albert Speer, a far more impressive figure within the Nuremberg dock. Just as the former Armaments Minister had once used his great organisational talents to maintain Germany's war effort, so now in the courtroom he deployed the skills needed to save his own skin. The projection of Speer's stoical moralism depended on conceding a measure of 'responsibility,' but hardly of criminal 'guilt.' How, he implied, could the Tribunal condemn a young architect who had simply been ensnared by the charismatic Fuhrer's flattery, and had fallen victim to that ethical tunnel-vision so pervasive among devoted technocrats?

This was a line of argument sufficiently insidious to prompt the British deputy prosecutor, Maxwell-Fyfe, into wondering privately whether Speer might be at heart a decent man who had been merely misled. Indeed, as things turned out, the plea succeeded in saving this prisoner from sentence of death. Such forensic resourcefulness was equalled only by Hermann Goring, albeit in circumstances where his status as the most prominent Nazi survivor made similar leniency unthinkable. From him especially, the familiar courtroom claim to have been ignorant of the Reich's genocidal practices rang utterly hollow. Yet, weaned from drugs, he did manage to rekindle at Nuremberg much of that shrewdness and intelligence which for long had made him Hitler's most powerful accomplice. At no point was this clearer than in March 1946, when, during Goring's cross-examination, it seemed to be he rather than Jackson, now the American chief prosecutor, who had the greater mastery over the documentary evidence and held the upper hand in much of their oral contest.

The Charges

More than half of those accused were charged under all four headings of the indictment submitted to the Tribunal. This document, encapsulating the prosecution's overall strategy, needs to be assessed with one eye on Simon's qualms. The American team concentrated on Count One concerning a 'common plan or conspiracy,' while the British focused on 'crimes against peace' under heading Two. Counts Three and Four, covering 'war crimes' and 'crimes against humanity,' fell to the Soviet and French lawyers who divided their labour according to the geographical emphasis of such offences in Eastern and Western Europe respectively. Attacks on the legitimacy of the Nuremberg proceedings are least convincing in regard to this latter pair of headings. We need to note particularly that, on the basis of massive documentary and photographic evidence concerning Nazi involvement in genocide and in the kind of atrocities thereafter symbolised by the names of such places as Lidice and Oradour, all but one (Streicher) of those eventually condemned to death were found guilty under Three and Four together.

Amongst all the charges, that of 'war crimes' had the strongest base in precedent. It built on the Hague Rules and the Geneva Conventions so as to deal with violations of law and custom during the actual conduct of hostilities. Thus Count Three explicitly condemned 'murder or ill-treatment' of civilians or prisoners of war, as well as 'killing of hostages, plunder of private property, wanton destruction of cities, towns or villages, or devastation not caused by military necessity.' The reference to 'crimes against humanity' under Four was more of an innovation. It reflected the prosecutors' need to adapt the war-crimes concept to conditions of total conflict in which barbarism had become systematised on a scale previously unimagined. The offence was defined as embracing 'murder, extermination, enslavement, deportation and other inhumane acts' and 'persecutions on political, racial, or religious grounds in execution of or in connection with any crime within the jurisdiction of the Tribunal.' Furthermore, international law was here extended to cover such acts even when they were committed against fellow-nationals—including in this case the wrongs which Germans had inflicted on Germans, whether Jewish or otherwise.

Flaws in the Conspiracy Charge

The Allies could have got most of what they wanted, and could have done so in a morally less dubious way, by limiting their prosecution solely to 'war crimes' and 'crimes against humanity.' However, as Simon had foreseen, the Americans were especially keen on a logic that emphasised how these actions had stemmed directly from the offence alleged under Count One—that of 'conspiring,' not least to unleash hostilities in the first place. Like the German defence counsel, the Soviet and French prosecutors made heavy weather of this concept. The judges eventually ruled that it could be pursued only when linked to 'crimes against peace,' and to events starting from November 1937 when some of Hitler's ideas about annexing Austria and Czechoslovakia had been recorded in the 'Hossbach memorandum.'

Yet this notion of conspiratorial plotting continued to influence all the proceedings. It encouraged the accusers to exaggerate the coherence of policy-making within Nazi Germany. Conversely, it spurred the prisoners into stressing the kind of organisational confusion that might assist their claims to have been ignorant about the worst horrors of the regime. Here the Nuremberg Trial heavily influenced future writing about the Third Reich. If the prosecutors tended to prefigure those 'intentionalist' historians who have seen the practice of Nazism as the relatively simple unfolding of certain deep-laid ideas, the defence provided a first sketch for some elements within those 'structuralist' or 'functionalist' interpretations which have put greater stress on constant improvisations of policy and on confusions of responsibility.

> *The gravest difficulties stemmed . . . from the involvement of the USSR at Nuremberg.*

That point is reinforced by the wrangles over Count Two. It condemned 'the planning, preparation, initiation, and waging of wars of aggression, which were also wars in violation of international treaties, agreements and assurances.' Thus the accusation knotted together many legal and historical complexities. It was easier to show the general aggressiveness of Hitler's foreign policies from 1933 to 1939 than to prove either that these sprang from what Jackson called a 'master blueprint' or that they were incontrovertibly criminal in substance. This was an area in which, as Simon had again warned, the law looked weak and the precedents seemed vague. In the absence of any international statute-making body, the accusers would have to rely heavily upon evidence that the states beyond Germany had actually behaved during the 1930s as though they already believed themselves to be confronting a criminal regime.

Here the Allied prosecutors faced numerous problems. For example, the Nazis' contempt for the League of Nations was doubtless deplorable. Yet Nuremberg's depiction of the organisation as a legal linchpin seemed merely hypocritical, granted that the USA had never joined it and that the USSR had even been expelled from it after attacking

Finland in 1939. Nor was there anything too convincing about the prosecution's frequent invocations of the Kellogg-Briand Pact of 1928. Did this not attract such wide formal support for its aim of renouncing war as an instrument of policy precisely by avoiding any actual definition of 'aggression' or any stipulation about penalties? Then, again, passages from Hitler's writings and speeches would be quoted in the courtroom so as to berate the defendants for their failure to see the criminal intent of his foreign policies, but no prosecutor ever directed the same harsh questions to those Allied 'appeasers' who had proved similarly blind. Concerning the 1930s, Schacht was surely entitled to enquire in his later memoirs: 'How were the German people supposed to realise that they were living under a criminal government when foreign countries treated this same government with such marked respect?' This was a point that E.L. Woodward, historical adviser to the British Foreign Office, was still making to the trial-planners on the eve of the Nuremberg proceedings, when he observed: 'Up to September 1st, 1939, His Majesty's Government was prepared to condone everything Germany had done to secure her position in Europe.'

The Allies' Crimes Undermined the Proceedings

This reluctant complicity by the Allies regarding certain Nazi policies that had been deemed criminal only in retrospect was not the worst potential flaw in the accusers' case. With reference to the indictment as a whole, it was understandable that those in the dock should also take every chance to register even more direct charges of tu quoque—that is, to stigmatise the unwillingness of the prosecuting powers to relinquish the privileges of 'victors' justice' by confessing to the crimes which they themselves had allegedly committed while fighting Hitler. The anxiety in Whitehall lest the defence should complicate Count Two by examining the Cabinet papers of 1939–40 that dealt with pre-emptive action over Norway (as an option possibly to be pursued even against any Norwegian resistance thereto) was a relatively minor matter. Far more serious was the vulnerability of the British, and the Americans, to counter-charges under heading Three. These involved allegations about 'wanton destruction' inseparable from those modes of aerial warfare against civilian targets which, even in the 1990s, continue to render controversial the name of 'Bomber' Harris, and indeed to cast doubt on the legitimacy of the atomic explosions detonated at the end of the conflict with Japan. This was one theme from the initial indictment which the prosecution soon found it prudent to soft-pedal, while another related to the waging of unrestricted submarine warfare in circumstances where Anglo-American practices turned out to be broadly similar to German ones.

The gravest difficulties stemmed, however, from the involvement of the USSR at Nuremberg. Such was the extent of its human losses in the war (on a scale being hugely revised upwards even today) that by 1945 any absence of Soviet prosecutors and judges had become even more unthinkable than their presence. Yet, as the representatives of one totalitarian system waxed eloquent in their condemnation of the vanquished leaders of another, there was every prospect of the USSR's participation severely weakening the moral and legal integrity of the proceedings. The cogency of Count Two, for example, was scarcely enhanced by the Nazi-Soviet Pact that Molotov had signed with defendant Ribbentrop on August 23rd, 1939. Indeed, the charge was substantially weakened by growing (and accurate) suspicion that the agreement must have carried some form of secret protocol granting the USSR an entitlement to launch its own acts of aggression against eastern Poland, the Baltic States and Finland.

Nor did Nuremberg benefit from the Soviet prosecutors' insistence upon specifying the massacre of Poles in the Katyn forest as a Nazi atrocity. By the close of the trial it was becoming plainer that the crime belonged not to 1941, as alleged, but to 1940 when the area was still under the control of the Red Army. By excluding from the final judgement all reference to this matter, the Western members of the Tribunal were paying silent and embarrassed testimony to the fact that in Eastern Europe, before as well as after Germany and the USSR became open enemies in June 1941, both the Nazi and the Stalinist regimes had pursued their irreconcilable goals with comparable ruthlessness.

On August 31st, 1946, the defendants made their own closing statements before the court, some showing defiance, others mere resignation at their expected fate. Over the next few weeks the members of the Tribunal completed their private deliberations, guided more by Lawrence's practical wisdom than by any flights of jurisprudential theory. From what we now know of these sessions, it is clear that, while some horse-trading between the judges became virtually unavoidable, they generally showed due care and fairness within the sometimes compromising framework of the Charter. The public reading of their findings began on September 30th. It ended the following afternoon with the announcement of their verdicts and sentences, which had been settled by simple majority vote whenever disagreement occurred. Acting probably on direct instruction from Moscow, the senior Soviet judge (General Nikitchenko) registered a last-minute dissent from the decision not to hang Hess, as well as from the three actual acquittals and from the Tribunal's selective approach towards deciding which Nazi organisations should be deemed criminal. In the early hours of October 16th—with seven defendants having been condemned to imprisonment, and with Bormann still missing—ten of the eleven remaining captives were duly hanged at Nuremberg. It was Goring who escaped the noose, by taking his own life via a cyanide capsule late on the previous evening. His corpse was simply added to the others roughly laid out in the prison gymnasium for the purposes of photographic record. All the bodies were then promptly transported to some unknown destination for a cremation and secret dispersal of ashes.

So concluded an enterprise which, even amidst the vengeful passions so understandable in 1945–46, had endeavoured to subject the Nazi tyranny to the cooler analysis of reason and of law. If political considerations too could not be entirely expunged from the proceedings, at least they were never permitted to become dominant. Soon the trial was providing a broad model for the legal action instituted by eleven Allied nations against Japanese leaders which started at Tokyo in May 1946, as well as for some later prosecutions in Germany conducted by individual occupying powers—most notably, by the Americans at Nuremberg itself until 1949.

Nuremberg's Success and Failure

The International Military Tribunal had proved largely successful in attaining its immediate objectives. True, the USSR had criticised what it saw as a lapse into leniency at the end, and elsewhere there was, in and beyond 1945–46, considerable public disquiet about those major weaknesses which we have noted within the prosecutors' case. Even so, though the latter imperfections could be exploited by those keen to purvey neo-fascist myths and legends, far fewer fantasies developed in Germany than had followed the defeat of 1918—and far fewer than would have flourished henceforth had the option of summary execution really been pursued. Who could ignore, above all, the contrast between the Tribunal's extended hearings and the peremptory conduct of 'justice' in the Nazi courts, let alone in the death-camps where even the pretence of legal process had been so murderously abandoned? In sum, the Nuremberg Trial played a very positive role in publicising the vicious origins, course, and consequences of Nazism, and thus in creating better prospects for democratic stability within the Federal Republic that would soon emerge from the zones of occupied Germany controlled by the Western Allies.

Yet those who organised the Tribunal placed no less store by their even broader aspirations for the decades ahead. Here the lack of success is something to which, half a century later, the state of our own world gives sad and ample testimony. Though by the end of 1946 the new United Nations had affirmed that the Nuremberg Charter and the concluding judgment should be entrenched as fundamental elements of international law, very little progress was made thereafter towards building on those strengths so as to establish a permanent court for the trial of relevant crimes. If Count Two depended on a dubious reading of the past, it had also represented an effort to mould a better law for the future. Another outbreak of world-wide conflict was certainly avoided during the long superpower confrontation of the Cold War, yet that perilous peace owed far more to mutual nuclear deterrence than to any lasting conversion to the rules promulgated at Nuremberg. Meanwhile, albeit on a sub-global scale, many 'crimes against peace' have been occurring—only for these aggressions to be left judicially unpunished.

3

The Rights of the Accused Were Protected at Nuremberg

Benjamin B. Ferencz

Those who simply wanted to see the Nazis punished for their acts during the war were not particularly concerned with the specifics of criminal procedure, but many thoughtful people were worried that the Nuremberg Trials would be a sham because the accused were so repugnant they would not be allowed to defend themselves. The trial was remarkably fair in the view of Benjamin B. Ferencz, who notes that the proceedings were open so that no one could accuse the major powers of conducting a secret trial and that any effort to railroad the defendants would have been plain to all. Ferencz suggests that the Allies made every effort to treat the Germans fairly, from allowing the defendants to choose their lawyers to providing their counsels with generous rations, salaries, and other perks. Most technical rules also favored the defendants or were adapted to insure their rights were protected, such as providing German translations of documents. Ferencz, a prosecutor at Nuremberg, believes that the results of the trial demonstrate that it was conducted in an impartial manner.

"He that would make his own liberty secure must guard even his enemy from oppression, for if he violates this duty he establishes a precedent that will reach himself." [Tom Paine] Since the trial of major war criminals by the first International Military Tribunal was completed in Octo-

From "Nurnberg Trial Procedure and the Rights of the Accused," by Benjamin B. Ferencz, *The Journal of Criminal Law and Criminology*, vol. 39, no. 2 (April 23, 1948). Reprinted by permission of the author.

ber 1946, twelve other cases have been presented in Nurnberg against German nationals charged with the commission of crimes against peace, war crimes, and crimes against humanity. Judgments have been rendered in eight cases, and the remaining four cases are in various stages of completion. . . . The Military Tribunals enforcing established international law were constituted in the American zone in pursuance of legislation enacted by the four occupying powers and similar tribunals were established in the other zones of occupation. That the crimes charged in these proceedings were punishable under preexisting laws has already been the subject of detailed examination and need not be here discussed. The landmarks in international law, which have been erected in Nurnberg, rest on a foundation of legal procedure that has satisfied the traditional safeguards of Continental and American law. The details of these rights and privileges, assuring a fair and impartial trial to each accused are but little known and worthy of consideration.

The facts that members of a defeated nation are tried in tribunals of the victor creates the need for closest scrutiny of the proceedings but does not necessarily or by itself render the conduct of the trials corrupt. Such processes are as old as war itself and have been conducted by the United States since George Washington ordered Major Andre tried as a British spy. Though the Nurnberg Tribunals, being international courts, are technically not bound by the laws of the United States, it is significant to note that the Supreme Court has recognized that the establishment of Military Tribunals to punish offenses against the Law of Nations is in full accord with Articles I and II of the United States Constitution. The Court pointed out that:

> An important incident to the conduct of war is the adoption of measures by the Military command not only to repel and defeat the enemy, but to seize and subject to disciplinary measures those enemies who, in their attempt to thwart or impede our military effort have violated the law of war.

In a later case, the Supreme Court stated that:

> The trial and punishment of enemy combatants who have committed violations of the law of war is thus not only a part of the conduct of war operating as a pre-

ventive measure against such violations, but is an exercise of the authority sanctioned by Congress to administer the system of military justice recognized by the law of war.

Following the many declarations made by the United Nations, which warned the Germans and held out hope and promise to the oppressed, it became the moral duty of the liberator not to forsake those pledges and to bring the criminals to trial. This became one of the very purposes of the war. Yet it is only a figure of speech to say, "the Vanquished are tried by the Victors." The individual offenders placed on trial are no more "Vanquished" than an ordinary criminal apprehended by police representing law-abiding society. The conflict that engulfed most of the world left no real neutrals whose interests were completely unaffected. . . . The proceedings of Nurnberg, though conducted by the United States, were always open to the German public. Correspondents and visitors from all parts of the world attended the trials without restriction or limitation. The written daily transcripts in German and English have always been available to anyone who cared about them. Where the complete record is readily available for the scrutiny or criticism of legal scholars the danger of tyranny is destroyed. The existence of American critics proves that there can be unbiased American judges. The judges were actually selected from prominent and respected members of some of the leading courts in the United States. Under such circumstances, the fact that the tribunals are composed of American jurists does not detract from the sincerity and fairness of the trials.

Military Government enacted legislation to ensure the rights of the defendants. A committee of the Presiding Judges of the Tribunals adopted rules of procedure consistent with the laws of Military Government and these rules were revised from time to time if it appeared that any hardship or difficulty of procedure existed.

Lawyers for the Defense

Every defendant has had the right under the law to be represented by counsel of his own selection, providing such counsel was qualified to conduct cases before German courts or was specifically authorized by the Tribunal. In practice this has meant that no German lawyer has ever been excluded if he was requested as counsel for a defendant. . . . Only three defendants requested American counsel. Two of these requests were promptly approved. The other, which was a request made late in the trial to have an American substituted for one of the German counsel who had previously been selected by the defendant himself, was disapproved. The Tribunal expressed doubt of the sincerity of the application when pointing out that the American was not, in fact, available. It was the opinion of the judges before whom he was to appear that the attorney had by his previous conduct defying orders of the Military Governor and by his violation of standing Military Government regulations disqualified himself. The right of a Tribunal to protect itself from abuse by unscrupulous practitioners is inherent in every court and in exercising that right in the one case, the Nurnberg judges made it clear that they did not intend to bar the defendants from the ethical employment of reputable American counsel. This same tribunal later approved American counsel for another defendant.

The proceedings of Nurnberg . . . were always open to the German public.

The solicitude shown the defendants is reflected in the privileges accorded their counsel. The highest number of prosecuting attorneys employed in Nurnberg for all trials was 75 as compared with the 191 German lawyers engaged for the defense. The United States Government provides a separate mess for the defense lawyers, where three adequate meals including American coffee are supplied. By command of the Military authorities all defense lawyers are given the largest German ration allowance, authorizing them 3900 calories daily, which is more than the amount received by American soldiers and almost three times the amount available to the average German. In addition, each one is gratuitously issued a very highly-prized carton of American cigarettes per week, which is a privilege afforded no employees of Military Government regardless of nationality or position. American air, rail, and motor transportation is authorized and American gasoline is given to those with private vehicles for their official use. Their salaries of 3500 marks per defendant are paid by the local Government and may be as high as 7000 marks per month as contrasted with the 200 marks received monthly by the average skilled worker. All needed office space for attorneys and clerical help is provided without charge. It may be fairly stated that the assistance given the Nurnberg defendants has been greater than that available to the average impecunious defendant in America.

Each defendant has the right . . . to present evidence in support of his defense, and may testify for himself.

The law requires that the indictment state the charges plainly, concisely and with sufficient particulars to inform the defendants of the offenses charged. At least 30 days must elapse between the service of the indictment and the beginning of the trial, and this has generally been exceeded. The time thus allowed for the defendant to prepare his case is greater than that required by German or American criminal or military law, and every defendant has received with the indictment German copies of all pertinent laws, rules and regulations.

Every defendant has the right to be present throughout the trial, which is conducted in German and English simultaneously by the use of interpreters and earphones. A sound recording of the verbal proceedings is made and used to check the accuracy of the translations and stenographic transcripts. These are promptly available to defense attorneys for use or correction.

Each defendant has the right through his counsel to present evidence in support of his defense, and may testify for himself, which is a right denied by continental law. All personnel, facilities and supplies for translation, photostating and mimeographing are available on equal terms to Defense and Prosecution.

Technical Rules

The Military Government Ordinance providing for the establishment of Military Tribunals specifically provides that the Tribunals shall not be bound by technical rules but shall admit any evidence which they deem to contain information

of probative value relating to the charges. Affidavits, interrogations, letters, diaries, and other statements may therefore be admitted. The opposing party is given the opportunity to question the authenticity or probative value of all
such evidence. Objection has been raised that this is broader
than the rules applied in courts of the United States and
therefore somehow deprives the defendants of a fair trial or
the due process of law required in American courts by the
5th Amendment. This question was brought before the
Supreme Court of the United States when the Japanese
General Yamashita was convicted by a military commission
where similar rules of evidence prevailed. The Court held
that Congress had authorized the establishment of such
rules by the Military Commander and they were subject
only to review of the Military authorities. No case has been
held to be unfair even though such rules have prevailed before British and American Military Commissions in the Pacific, Mediterranean and European Theaters and were in
fact provided for in the Charter of the International Military
Tribunal which was accepted and ratified by 23 countries
and affirmed by the General Assembly of the United Nations. Due process of law does not require any particular
type of tribunal so long as the proceedings afford the accused an impartial hearing and adequate safeguards for the
protection of his individual rights. Exclusionary rules of evidence arose in ancient Anglo-American common law to
prevent erroneous conclusions that might be drawn by a lay
jury receiving insubstantial proof. Where only judges skilled
in the law weigh the evidence, no such danger exists. The
numerous exceptions to the American "hearsay rule" admit
far more evidence than they exclude and no rule exists in
German law to exclude hearsay proof. The captured official
German documents, which constitute the bulk of the prosecution's case, have considerable probative value and to exclude such evidence that in many respects is more reliable
than the report years later of a prejudiced or emotional eye-
witness would be the height of folly. The weight given to
particular pieces of evidence varies, of course, with the nature of the proof, and the failure to impose rigid technical
rules on expert triers of fact and law in no way damages the
substantial rights of the defense. By ruling of the Tribunals
no document or exhibit may be offered against a defendant
unless a German copy has been given to his counsel at least

24 hours in advance. Usually the documents are furnished to the defense several days or even weeks in advance which is a privilege not accorded in German or American criminal or military courts. The accused may apply to the Tribunal for the procurement of documents on their behalf and these are brought to Nurnberg by the occupation authorities.

Where affidavits are admitted the opposing side may call the witnesses for cross-examination or if it is physically impossible for the witness to appear, cross-interrogatories or cross-affidavits may be submitted. The use of affidavits by the Prosecution has in fact been negligible as compared to that of the Defense and their admissibility has been an advantage to the defendants.

Each defendant, through his personal counsel, may cross-examine any witness called by the Prosecution and at his request the American authorities will transport to Nurnberg, feed, house and arrange payment for all witnesses for the defense. Prosecution witnesses share the same facilities, and once a witness is brought to Nurnberg, he may be interrogated freely by the side at whose request he was produced, or by the opposing side at whose request he was produced, or by the opposing side with the requesting party having the right to be present. There is absolutely no limitation on the defense concerning dealings with potential witnesses outside of the Nurnberg and all friends and relatives of the accused are free to act on his behalf. The only potential witnesses held in confinement by the Prosecution are those who cannot be released because they are subject to automatic arrest by the German authorities or are themselves awaiting trial. The methods employed in the interrogations have always been subject to scrutiny when the witness took the stand. There has never been a finding that force was ever employed by the Prosecution to obtain information from a witness or the accused.

Motions of either side are filed in both languages, with the adverse party having 72 hours in which to reply. At the conclusion of the trial, every defendant is allowed to address the Tribunal, which is a right denied by Anglo-American law.

Any defendant may call a joint session of the Military Tribunals to review any inconsistent ruling on legal questions which affect him, or any decision or judgment which is inconsistent with a prior ruling of another of the Military Tribunals.

The full opportunity given the accused to present their defense explains largely the duration of the trials. Invariably the defense takes much longer than the prosecution and in one case the defense lasted 72 days as compared with the prosecution's case of two days.

Results Show Fairness

The sentences actually imposed in the Nurnberg trials defeat the contention that they have been an instrument of vengeance. Germans, as well as Americans, have condemned the leniency increasingly shown by the Courts in these trials of major offenders. Of the 108 persons sentenced in the first seven cases, 20 were acquitted, 25 were sentenced to death, and in one of the most recent cases 5 high-ranking SS officers, who were convicted of membership in a criminal organization with knowledge of its criminal activities, were promptly released. The Tribunals have never exercised their power to deprive defendants of civil rights or to impose a fine or forfeiture of property, although it is almost a certainty that any defendant convicted by a German court would have been subjected to some or all of these penalties in addition to confinement.

Upon the completion of every trial the record of the case is sent to the Military Governor for review. He has power to mitigate, reduce or otherwise alter the sentence imposed, but he may not increase its severity. No death sentence may be carried into execution unless and until confirmed in writing by the Military Governor. The defendants have been given the privilege of sending petitions for review to the US Supreme Court and other high governmental offices. The Court has twice refused to review the Nurnberg cases, yet as of this writing no death sentence has been carried out though most of them were pronounced over six months ago.

It should be apparent to every unbiased critic that the good name of the United States has been upheld in Nurnberg by administering justice according to law and that those accused of war crimes [in the words of Robert Jackson] "have been given the kind of a trial which they, in the days of their pomp and power, never gave to any man."

4

A Measure of Justice

Neal Sher

In the mid-1990s, the criminal and civil trials of O.J. Simpson were the subject of incessant media coverage and hype. Revulsed by the notion that the Simpson murder trial had been the trial of the century, Neal Sher wrote about what he considered the real holder of that title—the Nuremberg Trial. He notes that the trial was not meant to exact justice for crimes against the Jews, an impossible task; nevertheless, a measure of justice was achieved for the victims. Neal Sher is a former director of the Justice Department's Office of Special Investigations.

It was just over 50 years ago—October 1, 1946—that the International Military Tribunal at Nuremberg delivered its historic verdict in the case that, by any standard, truly was "the trial of the century."

The significance of that proceeding was aptly and eloquently put forth by Justice Robert Jackson, the chief U.S. prosecutor at Nuremberg in his now-famous argument to the tribunal: "The wrongs which we seek to punish have been so calculated, so malignant and so devastating that civilization cannot tolerate their being ignored because it cannot survive their being repeated," he said. . . .

Virtually all of what has been written about the proceedings has focused on the main trial, in which Hermann Goering—who killed himself rather than face the hangman—was the most prominent criminal in the dock. Twenty-four defendants, high-ranking officials in Nazi Germany, were prosecuted for crimes against peace, war crimes, crimes against humanity and waging wars of aggression.

From "Real Trial of Century Was Fifty Years Ago, in Nuremberg," by Neal Sher, *Jewish Bulletin of Northern California*, November 8, 1996. Reprinted by permission of the author.

In addition, six Nazi groups and organizations—including the SS, the General Staff and the High Command of the German Army—were indicted as criminal organizations. Twelve defendants were sentenced to death, three to life imprisonment, three to lesser jail terms and three were acquitted.

As important as this judgment was, it must be understood that the trial was not convened to exact justice for the horrific crimes against the Jews. To be sure, the "Final Solution" entered into the proceeding, but it was far from the central focus.

In one of the subsequent and lesser-known trials, however, the mass murder of Jews figured prominently. In the so-called "Einsatzgruppen" case, the United States prosecuted 24 leaders of the SS mobile killing units, who were charged with the murder of 1 million people—mostly Jews—in the eastern occupied territories.

For the most part this savagery took place in 1941 and 1942, before the death camps were fully operational; the victims were shot to death by these "elite" units and their eager local collaborators. It is for good reason and without exaggeration that this case has been called the greatest murder case in history.

None of the Einsatzgruppen defendants showed any regrets or remorse.

One of the most astounding aspects of the case was the backgrounds of the defendants, who ranked from lieutenant to general. The presiding judge, Michael Musmanno from Pennsylvania, described the men responsible for such incomprehensible mass murder as follows: "The defendants are not untutored aborigines incapable of appreciation of the finer values of life and living. Each man at the bar has had the benefit of considerable schooling. Eight are lawyers, one a university professor, another a dental physician, still another an expert on art. One, as an opera singer, gave concerts throughout Germany before he began his tour of Russia with the Einsatzcommandos. This group of educated and well-bred men does not even lack a former minister, self-unfrocked though he was."

The overwhelming evidence consisted mostly of captured documents, which memorialized in grisly detail how these units, in town after town, city after city, "liquidated" the Jews. Most of the reports proudly noted that the areas of operation had been rendered "free of Jews."

Forty years later, these hair-raising documents were again relied upon in judicial proceedings. They were invaluable to the Justice Department's Office of Special Investigations, as they constituted ironclad proof of collaboration in mass murder by local paramilitary units, many of whose members had illegally immigrated here.

None of the Einsatzgruppen defendants showed any regrets or remorse. Some pathetically tried to claim that they were not aware of the murders and others relied on the "superior orders" defense.

The lead defendant, Otto Ohlendorf, was actually brazen and proud of his accomplishments, arguing that the massacre of Jews, even Jewish children, was a "military necessity."

"I believe that it is very simple to explain if one starts from the fact that this order did not only try to achieve security but also a permanent security, because for that reason the children were people who would grow up and surely, being the children of parents who had been killed, they would constitute a danger no smaller than that of the parents."

Fourteen of the 22 tried were sentenced to death; two were given life sentences; the others were given lesser jail time. One committed suicide.

Complete justice? Of course not. Anyone expecting full justice for the crimes committed against the Jewish people is destined for desperate cynicism. Complete justice could never, under any circumstances, be achieved. At least at Nuremberg there was some measure of it.

Chapter 3

Witnesses to History

1

Behind the Scenes at Nuremberg

Seymour Peyser

Though the defendants at Nuremberg were presumed to be guilty, the prosecutors went to great lengths to collect evidence to leave no doubt in the minds of either the judges or the public as to their crimes. This process was a massive undertaking that ultimately unearthed thousands of documents. Though the litigators are always the more glamorous attorneys in a trial, it is often the lawyers working behind the scenes to prepare the case that determine the outcome. Seymour Peyser was one of the lawyers responsible for preparing documents at Nuremberg. Among his jobs were to collect affidavits from the German police, judiciary, and press declaring the impact of Nazism on their lives and establishing the German chain of command to help prove who was responsible for actions taken during the war. In this excerpt from an interview with Peyser, he explains his job and what it was like to participate in the trial.

In 1933 Hitler comes to power. Were there no discussions at Harvard College and Columbia Law School?

It was the kind of discussion one would have about a distant country. Yes, I remember this clown that I had read about in the paper, [who] had suddenly become something to be serious about. Yes, he had this frightful anti-Semitism [which] was such an important part of his whole program and his whole being. Sure, Hitler was something that everyone learned to hate. He was the devil. But there was no in-

From an interview with Seymour Peyser, in *Witnesses to Nuremberg: An Oral History of American Participants at the War Crimes Trials*, by Bruce M. Stave and Michele Palmer, with Leslie Frank (New York: Twayne, 1998). Reprinted by permission of The Gale Group.

tellectual awareness of the size of this and I have looked back on it many, many times. It didn't really ring true to me until Nuremberg, until I got actually involved in reading and preparing for presentation. The size of it was something that shocked me and millions of others.

There were a few articles in the American papers—not much—and there were other articles in other magazines that I would occasionally get to look at. My parents were not politically conscious. I guess they would have been regarded as middle of the road and probably as Jews living in New York would have been regarded as Democrats. I knew that there were concentration camps and that this was a recurrence of the *pogroms* that had existed in Germany, Poland, and Russia and the kind of things that my grandparents had fled from, and that it was getting out of hand and getting to be enormous.

What transpired that brought you to Nuremberg?

Lots of things. How did I end up on Justice [Robert H.] Jackson's legal staff? Number one, in my first three and a half years in the army, I had started as a seventh-grade private and by the time Nuremberg started I was a major in the Judge Advocate General's department. . . .

I also had been editor of the *Columbia Law Review* and a good many of my predecessors and contemporaries on the *Law Review* had already in a few years distinguished themselves and they had applied and been selected. So the people that I think whose influence got me accepted were the late Harold Leventhal who had been the editor-in-chief of *Columbia Law Review* a year before my year (and before he died was a most highly respected judge in the Circuit Court of Appeals for the District of Columbia) and Ben Kaplan. Ben was one of the closest friends of Telford Taylor. It was chiefly on the recommendations of people like Harold Leventhal, Ben Kaplan, and a lawyer long gone, Warren Farr, with whom I had served in the army for a few months. . . .

It was in early August that we flew to Nuremberg and the trial started on the 20th of November. I was gone by Christmas, back home.

What preparation did you have to go over and what was it like when you first got there?

Preparation to go over, there was really none. I didn't speak German. I can bluff a little bit in a number of languages, but I knew that we had on the staff all kinds of translators and interpreters. I did some fast reading about the Nazis in a matter of weeks before I got onto a plane. . . . Somehow we got to London.

We lived in a drafty old place in Mayfair. The office was equally drafty. It was June, I remember. I remember shivering in June in London. I remember what we used to call Willow Run, which was the Grosvenor House main ballroom, served 3,000 meals to American army officers every day, stationed in and around London.

It was a strange time because the war in Europe was over and there was a kind of sighing of relief. It was a time of difficulties and shortages. Nobody had seen an orange in years. Here I was in the company of people I looked up to. I shook hands once in London with Justice Jackson. I only talked with him a couple of times in Nuremberg. He was quite aloof from the staff, but it was an opportunity for me to renew my acquaintance with Ben Kaplan, who was older, and Harold Leventhal, whom I knew well, and two or three others on the staff whom I had known, either in law school or at the JAG school or one way or the other, like Warren Farr.

The Americans were . . . the dominant operating group, but the British worked very much with the Americans.

We were planning our presentation, not knowing really very much about it. The only thing I could read in those days was the charter that had been agreed upon originally at the Potsdam Conference among Truman, Stalin, and Churchill. As Telford Taylor his book explains, there had been various plans. It was a monumental job to take the legal systems of four different countries, particularly with the Russian and French system being so far from the Anglo-American, and creating a system to try the major Nazi criminals. It wasn't clear in the beginning what they were going to be tried for, until the charter was fully written and approved. There were all kinds of problems, some of which had an impact on me, problems like who was going to represent and defend these 22 major Nazi defendants. That became an issue that wasn't decided until mid-October of 1945.

In London, what I did was to read as much as I could of

the work papers that had been prepared, many of them by the British, along with Telford Taylor, who had been one of the early leaders in working out the procedures. In many ways the fact that these four countries could work together was an achievement of great moment [in 1945], and that they could agree on a method of approaching the thing.

What most people still to this day forget is that these were military trials. This was a military tribunal and as far as the United States was concerned, it was convened by the president of the United States in his capacity as commander in chief, and the same is true of his majesty, King George VI. I don't even venture to know the origin of the authority in France or the Soviet Union.

I read as much as I could. Then I would get as much as I could of the translated writings of the Hitler group, so-called intellectuals of the Nazi movement way back to the *putsch* in Munich in the 1920s. And I read some of the so-called intellectual documents that had nothing to do with politics. This was the Aryan superiority. These were works of people like [Alfred] Rosenberg, like Robert Ley. Then I found myself in a plane on the way to Nuremberg. . . .

Germans in Denial

Did you have much interaction with the ordinary German public?

Very little in any kind of organized fashion. I remember we started out two different ways. I don't remember how, but I did visit a couple of families who lived in Nuremberg and I got a picture of what life was like. It was bleak. These were upper-middle-class people, I would guess. They spent most of the time in my presence justifying their existence and explaining how they were really not Nazis. This got to be a standard refrain whenever you would talk with a German. . . .

Nuremberg itself physically was something that had great effect on me. I don't know how much you have seen of the pictures of what Nuremberg looked like in 1945. It had been the target of a bombing attack on two nights [by] American and British bombers. The old city, which I had visited in 1930, [a] beautiful medieval city, was in ruins, just a mass of rubble, and people were living in that rubble. It was unsanitary, I'm sure, but these were Germans. These were not long-time homeless people. They were Germans and very proud of their ability to cope, and they had managed to create a little city in the ruins of the old buildings.

I didn't meet many Germans and I had some serious doubts as to whether I would want to. I don't know how many Jews were still around. I would think there were practically none still living in Nuremberg at the time.

It seemed to me to be appropriate [as a site for the trials] for a variety of reasons. For one thing, the big stadium was there, which had been the site for many of these enormous rallies that Hitler had. It had been the place for the so-called Nuremberg Laws, the [anti-Jewish] edicts that came out in Nuremberg at that time.

I was persuaded there was enough of a background to justify a trial.

It was a small city and from that point of view was difficult. It was not as big as Munich or Berlin or Frankfurt. It was literally a small town compared to them, and there weren't hotel facilities for all the visitors we had. Of course, nobody sat down to figure out this thing as a tourist attraction, but suddenly the tribunal found itself the center of all the media. God knows what would have happened in 1995, but in 1945 we had enough reporters to fill a whole castle, and that's where they lived, Walter Cronkite, Andy Logan who still writes for *The New Yorker*, a few others still around. The Faber Castle was where the press was located. The total staff was estimated to be almost a thousand, including 75 American lawyers.

Incidentally, [it was] as capable and as skilled a group of young lawyers as you could imagine at any time. For people like William Donovan and Sidney Alderman and Jackson, what they had already accomplished made their reputations. In the case of the others, consider what they were going to accomplish. Among 75 lawyers you had deans of law schools, many professors, many judges, presidents of the American Bar Association. [It was] quite a group. I had a gag that I used on another occasion: Of all these eminent people, I was the only one I never heard of. [laughs]

Painting a Picture

Was there a particular incident or an individual that stands out?

Yes, I'd say there were a couple of incidents in my few months in Nuremberg that stand out. . . .

One was in either late September or early October—I think it was September 1945. I worked directly under Ben Kaplan. My assignment was to deal not with the aggressive war path, but to paint the whole picture of the Nazi state and the Nazi party during the whole period before the war, beginning in the early 1930s until the time of the war, and gather in manageable form some evidence about what Hitler and what the Nazis had done to the judiciary, to the bar, to the press, to the police, to medicine, etc.

I remember sitting at a very early stage with Ben Kaplan in his office at the Palace of Justice and suddenly realizing that here we were as lawyers before a tribunal of judges who couldn't be assumed to know all of the things which we knew. It's the old problem of judicial notice that trial lawyers deal with regularly. We still had to prove what was the structure of the Nazi state and the Nazi party. How do you do that? To whom does box A respond, and when you get to that box A-1, where do you go from there?

The first job was, in effect, to draw a chart, find out what the whole organization was. We were helped immeasurably by the German mentality because they have always been so methodical and so precise about these things. They had the need to know, I guess, who each of them was responsible to. I had the assignment, given to me by Ben Kaplan, to draw a chart or to find a chart that we could present to the tribunal showing how the whole thing looked.

We learned right away that everything was in twos. There were the state and the party, and they were separate organizations, both, of course, led by Hitler. In the party he was the führer, in the state he was the chancellor. But he and his henchmen maintained this dual existence all along the line. So we looked it up and found, yes, the Germans did have charts of the state and the party. Trouble was that they were losing the war by 1943, 1944, and 1945 and they didn't bring their charts up to date. So how were we going to do that? How were we going to have it authenticated?

Someone came up with the proposition that Robert Ley, who was the head of the Labor Front, also had the title of vice president in charge of vice presidents—in charge of organization. Who better than he?

So we got him out of prison and following the required rules of the game at that time, I was in the Documentation Division, not in the Interrogation Division. Somehow or other the legal staff was divided between litigators and documentary organizers. I was in documentation. So we got Ley and arranged a meeting in a room next to the prison, and this is a day that stands out in my memory. It was in late September of 1945. I wasn't allowed to ask the questions, even though it was my job to prepare the chart. I had to bring along a lieutenant colonel from the Interrogation Division and I told him what questions to ask. He asked them and we sat next to each other. . . .

The Labor Leader

We traipsed into this room. Ley was 55 years old at the time. He had a bad cold, wore an off-white sweater that was unraveling at the elbow, and as we each came by, he clicked his heels and bowed. He immediately understood the insignia on my shoulder and he clicked his heels and bowed and said, "Herr Major." I had spent the night before reading some of the stuff he had written about the blood of the Jews running in the streets, incredible things, and I hated the son of a bitch. I remember that I had organized my intense feeling against him and he looked much older than 55 because he was ill.

So we sat down and started and we showed him the 1942 or 1943 charts. It was a series of the same questions. "Is that correct?" pointing to a box. Translated into German. "*Ya, das is richtig.*" Yes, that is correct. This went on. "*Nein, das ist nicht richtig.*" He said, "Well, because in 1944 we changed that and we put that department under this department."

We spent a good three hours with him because [there were] two big charts. The charts ended up on the wall of the courtroom. They were bigger than this whole wall and we ended up by being able to say that these had been authenticated by the top specialist in the Nazi hierarchy.

After we were with him two hours (everybody smoked in those days so he was getting a little bit flaky in his answers and you could see that his mind was really not all there), I handed him a cigarette, which he took immediately and lit, grateful for it. That cleared his mind so he could answer the next series of questions.

I realized suddenly that this was a human being. This guy was breathing badly because he had a bad cold. He wasn't a good specimen, but he was human and I no longer had that intensity of feeling that I had when I entered the room. I hadn't been trained for that kind of intensive long-time, stick-to-it hatred, and I have never forgotten that. . . .

Just to finish the story of Robert Ley—that night he killed himself. He hanged himself on a GI towel in the bathroom and the then-colonel in charge of the prison was transferred to a beat in Staten Island.

How did you feel when you heard that he committed suicide?

I wasn't sad. My immediate thought was, "Is that in any way going to affect the work we put into this?" I didn't have that kind of a feeling of concern for him; it's just that I wasn't good at this business of intense and continuous hating, which underlay the entire war for so many of us. I had a strong disgust for Ley, but here was somebody who was alive and then suddenly was not. In a human way I sympathized with this despicable man and said, "Well, he's better off." The remainder of his life was certainly not going to be a pleasant one and he would undoubtedly have been one of those with the most severe punishment. He would have been executed along with a number of them.

I don't think it was the greatest trial in history, but I think it was one of the great theatrical events of the judiciary.

But that was one story. The other, you asked generally for human stories. I guess that is one of the reasons for this process. The other was an interesting one. It had to do with the lawyers for the defendant. This being a military tribunal, if you took the standard operating procedure in American and I suppose British military law, the court-martial is convened by the commanding general, whoever that may be. In the case of the Nuremberg Trials it was Commander-in-Chief Harry S Truman. The prosecutor, known as the trial judge advocate, is appointed by that commanding general. Generally speaking, in military tribunals the defense counsel is also appointed, and under the Articles of War of the United States (and I assume similar rules in Britain), the defendant has the privilege of requesting civilian counsel, if civilian counsel is immediately available. It's a matter of convenience, again the decision [is] to be made by the commanding general, who is in this case the one who creates the trial.

Nazi Lawyers

The Americans and the British wanted to use the method used in our military tribunals because they were concerned that lawyers for these 22 characters, 22 defendants, would themselves be Nazis and we would be giving people prominence, simply as a professional matter, that they were not entitled to, and that it should be something that should be decided on a case-by-case method. There should be defense counsel and if the defendant makes a case for why he wants a civilian lawyer and a civilian lawyer is in other respects satisfactory, okay.

So the Americans and British went to a meeting in Berlin in October—early October, [or] late September. I was not there, obviously. This would only be, I think, the very top level of the organization; not only the chief of counsel, but representatives of the judges met with them on that occasion. The French and the Russians were violently opposed to this. They wanted the Germans to have their own lawyers because from the French point of view and to some extent I guess the Russians', they wanted to avoid the possibility that if the defendants exercised their choice or indicated their choice, they would invariably pick an American or a Briton and never a Frenchman or a Russian. So it ended two to two and that meant that the Americans and the British didn't feel that strongly about it.

It was decided that the defendants would retain their own counsel. They had, in many cases, the preeminent lawyers who were still alive. I remember the lawyer for Göring and for Schacht [was a] distinguished, elderly gentleman. All counsel wore the normal robes of a German lawyer, except for the lawyer for Admiral Dönitz, who was the assistant chief judge advocate of the German navy, who wore the uniform of the German navy into the courtroom until October 1946—one of the things that the Americans and British wanted to avoid. In any event, that's what happened.

What interested me was that we knew, sitting in Nuremberg, that this was a subject of dispute and had not been fully decided. It occurred to me that I might be facing a problem. One of the first things I had done when I reached Nuremberg, before I got onto this business of the structure of the state and other interesting jobs which I had, [was] to go over the list of all the roles that Hermann Göring had had and prepare a definitive list of them and have him sign off that these were the jobs that he did, which I did. He had some 25 or 30 different roles during the Nazi period, during that 15-year period. Therefore, I was a little bit more up on Göring than some others of us, [although] certainly not as much as those who had studied this as a life work.

Here I am late one evening in the bar at the Grand Hotel considering what would happen if Göring said, "That's him. I want that lawyer. I want an American Jew representing me." It might have been an offbeat kind of thing, but it was conceivable. He was clearly the brightest of the defendants, nobody ever doubted that. He didn't doubt it and none of the other 20 who were there doubted it. . . .

Anyway, what would have happened? It wouldn't have been possible for me to say, "Well, I'm sorry but I won't do it." I'm in the army. This could be an order. As it happened, I thought about it considerably because in Manila at about the same time or a little after, an old friend of mine, Frank Riel, had been ordered by General [Douglas] MacArthur to defend [Japanese General Tomoyuki] Yamashita and he had not wanted to. He had been told by his senior commanders, "What you want to do is not relevant here. Do it." And he did. . . .

At any rate, it was a purely theroretical thing and never did happen, but many times I thought to write something along those lines, a fictitious treatment.

Again, by lucky accident, I was general counsel of United Artists Corporation in the 1950s and in that capacity served as a kind of technical advisor to Stanley Kramer on *Judgment at Nuremberg*. . . .

Is it fair to say that the Americans were running the trial?

No, it's not fair. They were certainly the dominant people. I would say the Americans were the host country and they were the dominant operating group, but the British worked very much with the Americans, and the British had some very competent and very hard-working lawyers. The French lawyers were bookish, professor types who never seemed to be getting out into the real world. The Russians seemed impatient and wanted to get on with the hanging. Everything that they did thereafter made that clear. . . .

No Innocents

Was there in general a presumption of guilt?

Yes, sure there was. A presumption in feeling, but you got American and British lawyers who are trained to think otherwise. The fact that three of the defendants were acquitted is an indication that that meant something. The Russians certainly didn't vote for acquitting Fritzsche. He was the head of the radio section of the press under Goebbels. You know why he was one of the 21 charged with being principal criminals? Because he was one of the few people that the Russians had captured. He was captured in their zone and they had him physically and everybody else had been dug up by the victorious people from the other countries.

How could the four powers stand in judgment when the Russians were already starting their takeover of the Balkan States and the French had violated the Geneva Convention by mistreating prisoners?

It was more than just that. We knew of particular incidents where the Russians particularly had been involved. Yes, there was a sense of unease, but not very much we could do about it except go through with it. We couldn't stop in the middle and say, "Well, one of our victorious countries is also guilty. Would they please stand in the dock?" Yes, we knew about it. . . .

What's your feeling about Nuremberg justice?

My feeling, very frankly, was that I was persuaded there was enough of a background to justify a trial and that it was much better to go through this process. Certainly there was enough evidence under the classic war crimes definitions, the rules of land warfare, as it's called. Nobody could object to the evidence that American prisoners and American hospital workers and medics had been dealt with in violation of the old conventions going back to the beginning of the twentieth century.

The important thing is that they added two other basic counts. One was the planning and waging of an aggressive war. This bothered a lot of people who felt they were being more realistic saying that the victors in any war are going to claim that the vanquished were trying to wage an aggressive war. The Serbs are now doing the same thing, so I can understand that argument.

The final one, which is what I think has interested the

people of the world and the media, is the crimes against humanity. There's no precedent for people being tried for this. . . .

Public Perceptions

When you returned to America, did you have the sense that people in the U.S. understood what was happening in Nuremberg?

No, because many thinking people were asking similar questions about *ex post facto* justice. I don't think that many of them knew about the Katyn massacre [in Russia in the spring of 1940] that the Russians were guilty of. I don't think that was common knowledge, or that the French had been guilty of violations of the traditional war crimes conventions.

This was a pretty big show. It was not so much the importance of it as, you know, you've got this incredible guy, Göring. To be sure there would be nothing comparable if it had been on television. . . . But you had Göring, with his jowls hanging down. He had lost 100 pounds, was very bright, listening and taking advantage of every question, every translation. He understood English very well and therefore had a great advantage.

I was told by people who were there and whom I respected that Göring toyed with Jackson. Jackson made the mistake of asking questions when he did not know what the answer was going to be. You had him and you had this mask-like face of Rudolf Hess sitting right next to him, and you had a bunch of small, evil men like Rosenberg and Streicher and Sauckel, all of whom were really directly involved in genocide.

You also had the generals and the admirals, an entirely different cast of characters. You wondered how they allowed themselves to get into this thing and by the same token, you realized that they never had been trained to avoid it. They just did what came naturally to them. This is quite a cast, in many ways much more exciting as a theatrical attraction than *Judgment at Nuremberg*. Even more exciting than Spencer Tracy. . . .

Was Nuremberg the greatest trial in history?

I don't think it was the greatest trial in history, but I think it was one of the great theatrical events of the judiciary in that area.

I think with all of its limitations, and it certainly had many, and all of the errors that were made there, I think the world is better off that these four countries did what they did, rather than shooting all the defendants.

Any human venture can be said to be futile in an absolute way. Of course the judges are people with feet of clay. Of course the judging countries are defective, as ours will always be. It's not by itself the greatest trial in history. It's not itself going to prevent other aggressive wars or other unspeakable genocides, but it's something that can be used to mobilize people and persuade people.

2
A Prosecutor's View

Drexel Sprecher

Reading most accounts of the Nuremberg Trial, it is possible to learn about the debates associated with who to try and how to try them, the results of the trial, and some opinions about the influence of the event on history. To learn about the arguments and politics behind the scenes, however, it is usually necessary to find firsthand accounts of the trial or memoirs by the participants. General histories usually do not offer impressions of the major figures or reveal mistakes they made. Court TV interviewed prosecutor Drexel Sprecher and obtained some of these inside stories. This excerpt provides a glimpse of the good, the bad, and the amusing aspects of the trial.

QUESTION: What were your expectations of the Nuremberg Tribunal?

SPRECHER: My expectations of the Nuremberg Tribunal was not only that it would punish some of the worst criminals of all time, but also that it would expose in a way that people could understand how a dictatorship came to power, and how it slowly built itself to be the oppressive regime it was.

QUESTION: . . . Were your expectations fulfilled? . . .

SPRECHER: I think for the most part they were. For some time after the trial, I was a little surprised that the public attention had been diverted by one thing and another. Particularly by the Cold War. But oh, for the last 20 or 30 years, I think there's been a renewed interest. . . .

QUESTION: Why did Justice Jackson concentrate on the notion of aggressive war?

From an interview with Drexel Sprecher by Court TV, published at www.courttv. com/casefiles/nuremberg/sprecher.html. Copyright © 1999 by Courtroom Television Network LLC. Reprinted with permission.

SPRECHER: Well, I think that Justice Jackson concentrated on aggressive war because it encompassed the whole. The atrocities, the war crimes, would not have been possible if there hadn't been aggressive war.

So I think he wanted to point out and to emphasize that the worst crime of all is the initial one, which is aggressive war. And that following it come the atrocities and the war crimes. . . .

QUESTION: Now, what were Justice Jackson's expectations of Nuremberg? How did he see it?

SPRECHER: Well, I expect that he saw it as a great means of exposing the Nazi regime as well as a means of getting the punishment of the main leaders.

QUESTION: Now, did his attitude about the tribunal change at all during the trial, during the course of the trial?

SPRECHER: About the tribunal in the sense of the judges or the whole proceeding?

QUESTION: Both. First talk about the judges. How, what were Jackson's impressions of the judges?

SPRECHER: Well, I know very little about what his impressions of the judges were, because he never talked to me about it. So I can't really give you much help there.

As far as the tribunal is concerned, he began to get worried after the defense case began that the tribunal was allowing the defense too much leeway. And that they weren't paying attention to relevancy or accumulation.

So at one point, he gets into quite a struggle with the tribunal, which was most unfortunate. And he lost his temper. And that was most unfortunate, too. Because he was not given to that normally speaking. And I don't think he ever lost it again. . . .

Challenges to the Prosecution

QUESTION: What were the biggest problems that the U.S. prosecutors faced at Nuremberg?

SPRECHER: Well, I would say the first big problem was that we didn't have enough German speaking people there. Very few of the attorneys themselves spoke German.

And accordingly they had to rely on research analysts. And there weren't enough good research analysts to both do the finding of the documents and then their translation.

So we had a translation bog down during the first part of the trial, which was most unfortunate. And had we done what we later did under Lt. Col. Peter Eberal, and sent a whole team to England to have recruited more German speaking people of the first rank, we would have saved ourselves a lot of grief at the beginning of the first trial.

QUESTION: And as the trial went forward, as the first trial went forward, what other challenges did the U.S. prosecutors face?

SPRECHER: Well, one of the main problems of the prosecution overall was that there wasn't any great correlation between the four delegations. There was between the Americans and the British, partly because Sir David Maxwell-Fyfe was such a wonderful diplomacist, and a man of unusual ability and character.

But the relations with both the French and the Soviets were not that close that you could work things out very well. Had their been one overall Chief Prosecutor who could have pulled things together, it would have saved a lot of time. And there wouldn't have been as much repetition.

QUESTION: . . . Did the Soviet prosecutors perceive Nuremberg as just another political show trial?

SPRECHER: No, I don't know what you mean by another political show trial. I think they had a great interest, a very genuine interest in having exposed what happened. Because after all, they had lost more people than anybody else had lost, due to the Nazi invasion, and due to the occupation practices after that. So they had a very good reason to want a very full exposition.

The major difference was that they tended to rely themselves on official reports, some of which were good, and some which were a little distended by prosecution type language, you might say.

Whereas our idea was to rely as much as possible on the contemporaneous German documents.

And as the trial went along, I think the Soviets learned more from that. And for that matter the French did too.

Allied Divisions

QUESTION: What were the goals of the French at Nuremberg?

SPRECHER: Well, they mainly wanted to expose what had happened to the countries in the west during the German occupation. And the main difficulty was that they were so overcome and overwhelmed by the defeat and their government hadn't really been reconstituted well.

And they sent all kinds of miscellaneous things to Nuremberg which hadn't been certified. And it was very difficult for us to get them to follow Anglo-Saxon standards in getting their documents and their other proof together. And I think some of them did. But some of them were still kind of learning about the process.

You see, there's a difference between continental law and the Anglo-Saxon law. In the continental law, the prosecutors tend to pour in their materials. The judge looks it all over. And then the judge takes the leadership in questioning and so forth.

The main problem [with] the conspiracy charge was that we made it too broad.

That's quite different than in the Anglo-Saxon process, where the judge knows practically nothing before the trial starts. And it's up to the prosecution to do all the leadership in presenting the evidence.

QUESTION: What about the conspiracy charge? Wasn't that a new notion to the French and Russian and German lawyers at Nuremberg?

SPRECHER: Well, partly it was. The main problem, in my view, [with] the conspiracy charge was that we made it too broad. And we said the Nazi conspirators, meaning all the men in the dock, plus some others, did so and so.

Now, as a matter of fact, there were very great variations among the defendants and others as to what they did, and why they did it.

And the tribunal cut the conspiracy charge back a great deal, and had it start in November, 1937. And they found only ten of these defendants guilty. And many other people, of course, were therefore not involved at all in this narrower conspiracy. Our mistake was making too broad a conspiracy charge.

The French, the Germans and the Russians have some notion of conspiracy, but it's a much more limited one than ours was. And so the final result was closer, moved more in their direction and less in the Anglo-Saxon direction than was the case at the beginning of the trial.

Errors in Judgment

QUESTION: What were the mistakes that were made at Nuremberg?

SPRECHER: Well, there were several very large mistakes. In the first place, the accusation that the Nazi leaders, the Nazi regime, had committed the Katyn massacres [the massacre of several thousand Polish Army officers in 1943 by order of Stalin]. That was pushed upon the prosecution during the last couple days before the indictment was filed, when they were assembled in Berlin and waiting to file the indictment with the judges.

And the other prosecutors, the Americans and the British, should have objected. But they didn't have the details. And besides, they were under some pressure. As a result, the Soviets got away with it. And it was put into the indictment.

At the trial, after the Americans and the British and the French began to see that this was probably a very clouded thing, they refused to put in any evidence or to mention it in any way. When the tribunal came to write its judgment, the Katyn matter is not mentioned one bit either. So it just fell out of the case. But it was a disturbing element.

QUESTION: What were some of the other mistakes?

SPRECHER: Well, one of the other mistakes was the indictment, in my view, of Hjalmar Schacht. Schacht had indicated some variations from Goering which were rather substantial, before the war. And then he'd gone into almost complete retirement.

Jackson became angry. And he showed it. And that was most unfortunate.

During the last part of the war, he undoubtedly had some connections with some of the conspirators who attempted to take the life of Hitler on July 20th, 1944. Now, how close those were, we don't know. Schacht maybe later blew it up a bit.

But it was very clear that we had not gone sufficiently into Schacht's background. After all, Hitler had him thrown in concentration camps nearly a year before the trial began. And he was in several concentration camps. Because Hitler thought he was guilty of having conspired against Hitler. Well, that's not the kind of a man to put in the dock, and we made a mistake.

Camp Films

QUESTION: Were you present in the courtroom when the concentration camp film was introduced?

SPRECHER: Yes.

QUESTION: What was the atmosphere in the courtroom like when the concentration film was shown? And what was the reaction to it?

SPRECHER: Well, the concentration camp film had been put together by a good friend of mine, Jim Donovan, from the Office of Strategic Services. So I'd even seen parts of it beforehand. I was not particularly surprised at what was shown.

But the horrors of seeing the bodies stacked up and the ditches and the movement of so many people onto trains and into the concentration camps was a shocking thing to see. And it affected the audience very much. You could feel it at the time it happened.

I think everybody had the sense that . . . we were helping make history.

QUESTION: How did the defendants react?

SPRECHER: Well, I was busy watching the film at the time. And of course, the court was, the lights were different during that showing otherwise. So I don't know. But I think Speer revealed . . . later that he thought this is one of the things that helped him create some division among the defendants. Because it was so obvious that the Hitler regime had committed some of these horrible atrocities associated with the concentration camps.

QUESTION: Why was the film introduced?

SPRECHER: I think as a dramatic way of showing some of the evils that had happened. I think it was, it was perfectly legitimate to show the film for that purpose.

QUESTION: Do you think the U.S. case was too reliant upon documents?

SPRECHER: No. I don't think that the U.S. case was too reliant upon documents. I think that at first, Jackson probably wanted to use documents and have very few witnesses. But he was persuaded that he ought to have at least several. And so we had several very good prosecution witnesses.

QUESTION: . . . Why was he persuaded to have witnesses? What were the arguments?

SPRECHER: I think one of the main things was to get a break in the trial. And just avoid the constant repetition of things about documents. And that the live witnesses kind of brought the whole thing to life in a way that the documents did not.

QUESTION: Why did the U.S. prosecute the Nazi organizations?

SPRECHER: The hope in prosecuting the Nazi organizations was that it would save a lot of time in prosecuting individuals. . . . Again, I think there we went a little far, as the tribunal pointed out in its findings. What we were attempting to do is make a prima facie case, which would be very difficult for defendants in later trials to rebut.

But the tribunal said the prosecution must prove that the defendant in a later trial knew these things that went on about the . . . particular organization that was accused of being criminal.

The tribunal also threw out three of the cases . . . that we had; we had indicted the Reich Cabinet, that was thrown out. We had indicated the Storm Troops, the S.A., that was thrown out. A lot of people were worried about that one, but when you look back at it, the S.A. had had such an up and down history that it probably was just as well that it was thrown out. . . .

The Defense

QUESTION: What are your thoughts on Jackson's cross-examination of Goering?

SPRECHER: I think most of his cross-examination was very good. A lot of the things he got Goering to admit and to come out with during the first part of his exam was very good. But as he went along and tried to pin Goering down, he began to ask questions which kind of irritated Goering. And Goering started to give him very long answers.

Jackson became angry. And he showed it. And that was most unfortunate. And that's the only time I remember him getting angry in court. He never got angry when he cross-examined Schacht, nor when he cross-examined Speer. He kept his temper very well and did a good job.

QUESTION: Do you believe the defendants at Nuremberg received an adequate defense?

SPRECHER: I think that the defendants at Nuremberg received a very adequate defense. They had some very good counsel. I think Otto Kranzbuehler is one of the brightest counsel I've seen anywhere. He was very clever in the way he presented the case of Doenitz. And by getting an affidavit from Admiral Nimitz, our Admiral Nimitz, he in effect made the prosecution back up on some things.

I do think that [Nuremberg] is only beginning now to fulfill its true legacy.

And the finding with respect to illegal and unrestricted submarine warfare is a very restricted one. Had largely to do with the shooting of survivors after the submarines had been sunk and so forth. So—he was one example.

The other thing is, the other good example is Dr. Rudolf Dix, who was the President of the German Bar Association, before the Nazis came to power. And I think he was a very capable lawyer. There were a number of others who were very good lawyers. . . .

Inside the Court

QUESTION: Tell me about the first time you walked into the courtroom?

SPRECHER: The first time I came into the courtroom during the trial was just before the defendants were brought into the dock. And as they were brought in by a guard, one by one, and sat down where they knew they were going to sit, because there had been a preview for them, as I saw them coming in there, I could hardly really believe it's finally happening. And I must say, tears came to my eyes.

QUESTION: Had there been a lot of delays before the trial started?

SPRECHER: No. There hadn't been any particular delays before the trial started. We were very crowded, but once the indictment was served, I don't think anybody had any desire to have the date of trial moved backward or forward. They wanted it to come off just as it had been set forth.

It pushed us a good deal, but it really came off very well.

QUESTION: Was there a sense of history about it? Did you have the sense that you were making history?

SPRECHER: I think everybody had the sense that, what with the documents we had, and what with the drama of the trial, we were helping make history, and that we were doing it in a way which would call attention to many more people than could possibly be done if there had been no trial. . . .

QUESTION: What were your impressions of Judge Lawrence?

SPRECHER: Judge Lawrence was one of the most amazing people I ever hope to see on the bench or off the bench. He had a firmness about him, and yet he didn't sound, nor did he behave in an arbitrary fashion. And he seemed to listen and remember great amounts of detail as to what had gone on before, and what had been said.

And when he was wrong, he didn't hesitate to admit it. I think that between him and Sir David Maxwell-Fyfe, and Justice Jackson, you have the three big characters of the trial. . . .

Outside the Court

QUESTION: What was the atmosphere like in Nuremberg outside the courtroom?

SPRECHER: Well, of course, the, the Germans at the time, or particularly during the early part of the trial, were having such a difficult time in getting enough food to subsist on. And Nuremberg had tremendous numbers of the people in the center of Nuremberg who had moved out to the suburbs or some distance away because of the heavy bombing and the heavy shelling of Nuremberg.

They started to come on back in. And you would begin to see more Germans walking up and down the streets. And clearing the great debris, and clearing the streets and so on. There was a lot of jobs that were created for the Germans. And accordingly, the, the—downtrodden appearance of the average German tended to become less apparent. And they began more and more to look like restored human beings.

QUESTION: What was the attitude of the German people toward the trial?

SPRECHER: I think it was—there was a set of different attitudes, in that they changed as the trial went on. At the beginning, I think a lot of the Germans felt this is just the victors over the vanquished kind of thing.

But when they began to see that there were not only defense counsel, but that the German witnesses were testifying about what they had experienced, which showed crimes by the Nazi regime, then I think there tended to be a great change and a great more receptivity to listening to what was going on at the trial, both by radio and through the newspapers. . . .

Speer's Surprise

QUESTION: What was the most unexpected thing that happened during the trial to you?

SPRECHER: I suppose that one of the most unexpected things to me only partly showed up at the trial. And it came out partly when we heard that Speer was going to assume a certain collective guilt, because he had been associated so intimately with the regime that had done many things.

And even though he was going to say I didn't know some of the details of the horrors, he was going to take some responsibility for that. I suppose when that began to come out, during his testimony, that was as surprising a thing to me as happened during the trial.

One of the legacies of Nuremberg was to make us look more at potential dictators and to try to nip them in the bud.

QUESTION: What did you expect that Speer would do?

SPRECHER: Well, I hadn't known of him personally to speak of at all. I probably had been at an interrogation before the trial. But it never struck me as it had the prison psychologist, Dr. Gilbert. Dr. Gilbert damn well knew that Speer was going to assume responsibility for quite a few things.

But we never had any contact with Dr. Gilbert during the trial. He stayed away from the prosecution like mad. . . . He wanted to keep that role, so that he could say to the defendants, look, I'm your psychologist. And nobody else's.

Now that his book has been out many years, I've seen how it corroborates what Speer was thinking. He built a kind of an opposition to Goering within and among the defendants, which was really quite substantial. It even effected one of my two defendants, Von Schirach. Von Schirach came around and finally made the statement, "I have led millions of German youth to serve a barbaric master.". . .

The Rule of Law

QUESTION: Nuremberg has been called a meaningless triumph of international law. Do you agree?

SPRECHER: No. I don't agree at all. I do think that it is only beginning now to fulfill its true legacy, its full legacy. Because there have been conferences all over, and a tremendous number of legal professionals have thought about the trial and its implications. And how it is different than the situations which have arisen since.

I mean, in Bosnia we just don't have physical possession. We haven't captured the leading defendants. In Nuremberg, we had them all. So, it made a lot of difference. I, of course, think that they should have indicted the top Serbian leaders months ago, and tried them in absentia, in their absence. If they had notice, they could come. And if they didn't want to come, why we'd use what evidence we had.

And I think it would have stopped some of the crimes which have been committed since. And that it would have given a good leeway, a good headstart on having some further trials now.

QUESTION: Do you think the rule of law can be effective after a trial in which the defendant isn't present?

SPRECHER: Well, take the case of Bormann in the first trial. He was tried in absentia. He was the closest man to Hitler during the last couple of years of the war. This was brought out very clearly. And had he been there—of course, he was dead we found out later. We weren't sure at the time we indicted him.

But had he wanted to bring out evidence, and had he been alive, he could have done this. If, by sending letters or by sending materials to his counsel. Or he could have insisted on being present. . . .

Letting Them Off Lightly

QUESTION: Are there any defendants you think were treated too lightly by the tribunal?

SPRECHER: Yes. I—I think that Fritzsche, the defendant I prosecuted, he was clearly a man down at the third level. And he shouldn't have been in the dock, because of that reason. But after he was there, I think that the tribunal could have tied together the infuriating statements he made concerning Jews and capitalists and imperialists and so on, and found that he also contributed to the will of the total Nazi regime to liquidate Jews.

The difference between his case and the Streicher case was that Streicher had read a Swiss newspaper, the "Israeleidische Volkenblacht" in which it talked about the removal of the Jews to the east, and that they were disappearing and not being heard of again. And he printed this from the "Israeleidische Volkenblacht" and then he said, this is no goddamn Jewish lie. Well, there we had proof that he knew that they were being eliminated in the concentration camps. This was pretty thin in the case of Fritzsche. But he had been behind the German armies when they went into the Soviet Union and when a million people had been killed.

He had been right next to Von Neurath, who was right next to Goebbels, who certainly knew. And why didn't he do a little more inquiring in order to find out what was happening to these thousands upon thousands of Jews that he knew were being taken out of Germany, Austria, and other places? Why didn't he?

I thought he could have been found to have been criminally negligent in that regard. The tribunal just wanted more proof on that than we gave them. And so he was found not guilty.

QUESTION: Do you think the tribunal treated Speer too lightly?

SPRECHER: I think that all depends. I think Speer was as responsible as Salko was for the fact that so many slave laborers were drawn into Germany. But I think the tribunal was moved by the fact that Speer was more contrite, and that he was more open.

And I can't help but think that that was one of the reasons why they reduced his sentence to 20 years. And I'm very glad they did. Because Speer has produced at least two books, "Inside the Third Reich," and the book about Spandau, which are tremendous contributions to world history. . . .

QUESTION: Were there any defendants who you felt the tribunal treated too harshly?

SPRECHER: No. I—I didn't feel that they treated any defendant too harshly. . . .

QUESTION: Did it trouble you at all that these defendants were executed?

SPRECHER: No, it didn't. And now that has an interesting reflection back on my past, because I was against the death penalty as a student at the University of Wisconsin.

But when I began to hear about the Nazi crimes, and their extent, it did seem to me that it would be very bad to let most of these people survive all this and not to make the world know that they had paid for it with their lives. So I had a change of mind about the death penalty in that respect. . . .

The Trial's Legacy

QUESTION: What is Nuremberg's legacy?

SPRECHER: Well, I think it's a multiple legacy. I think the legacy of Nuremberg is partly to make people think at an earlier point about potential dictators and how they themselves get tied into a regime which begins to take shortcuts, and which sooner or later starts to kill its opposition. First some of its own people.

As Justice Jackson said, the first victims of the Nazi regime were the German people. And then he went out and spread to other folks.

I think one of the legacies of Nuremberg was to make us look more at potential dictators and to try to nip them in the bud at a sooner rate.

Another thing about, another part of the legacy would be we need to have a permanent establishment that is ready to go and hunt war crimes and develop materials on war crimes very early, and not have to put together a last minute group of people.

Now, I think we did reasonably well at the end of the war, because we had so much money and people were so anxious to do things. . . .

Lighter Moments

QUESTION: What was the funniest thing that happened during the trial?

SPRECHER: Well—one of the funny things that happened during the trial is right on the record. A fellow by the name of Von Steingracht who was one of the number two men in the Foreign Office, was on the stand.

And he was asked by Col. Aman if he hadn't been at Ashkan. Now, Ashkan was the name of a detention center where many of the defendants had been. And when Aman asked him about that, the translator translated, now you were in an a—you were incarcentrated in an ash can. And he says, no, I was never incarcentrated in an ash can. And there was just this missing of the words in the translation. And the whole audience burst into laughter. And Lord Lawrence had a hard time not laughing himself.

And I'm told that after a while, when he got in chambers, that he laughed like mad as, as well.

QUESTION: Nuremberg has been criticized as being an instrument in which laws were applied retroactively to crimes that had already been committed. How do you respond to that?

SPRECHER: Well, the ex post facto argument has some relevance with respect to crimes against the peace. However, from 1899, 1906 and later, at the Hague, there was a Hague convention, and the Geneva convention, which proscribed certain things which are not to be done during wars, or treatment not to be given to prisoners of war and so forth.

So there was that body of international law that existed with respect to what we called strict war crimes. The idea that there was a crime against the peace requires, when it seems to me to go to the Kellogg-Briand pact of 1926, which was called the Pact to Outlaw War. . . . But it didn't prescribe criminal penalties. So . . . the charter at Nuremberg was a build on to that in the sense that it provided a tribunal, and a means of prosecuting persons who had . . . been a part of committing the crime against peace.

3

The Hangman of Nuremberg

Jon Marcus

Though the inclination of many Allied officials after the war was to execute all the prominent Nazis, the decision to hold a fair trial posed the risk that some of the defendants might be found not guilty. Of the twenty-two defendants, an even dozen were convicted on all charges and sentenced to death. Of those, two escaped the penalty; Goering committed suicide, and Bormann was never caught. The method chosen for those to be executed was hanging, which meant there had to be a hangman. No one was forced to carry out the sentences; instead, a call went out for volunteers. Joseph Malta stepped forward. Associated Press writer Jon Marcus interviewed Malta fifty years afterward and found he had no regrets.

One at a time, they dropped through the trap door of the hangman's scaffold and fell still.

Gestapo boss Ernst Kaltenbrunner. Hans Frank, governor-general of occupied Poland. Slave-labor czar Fritz Sauckel. Austrian Nazi Arthur Seyss-Inquart.

In all, 10 of the men who led the Third Reich were hanged in Nuremberg on October 16, 1946, for crimes against humanity.

"It was a pleasure doing it," said 78-year-old Joseph Malta, the U.S. Army military policeman who pulled the lever. "I'd do it all over again."

Malta hanged 60 Nazi government and military leaders but became known as Hangman 10 for executing 10 top Nazis on that one night in the gymnasium of Nuremberg's Landsberg Prison.

"These were the ones that gave the orders," he said. "They weren't sorry for anything."

Malta was a 28-year-old MP when the Army asked for volunteers to hang the men condemned by the International Military Tribunal. He stepped forward, he said, because he had learned during his short time in occupied Germany about the Nazis and their newly exposed crimes.

"Being there and talking to the people there, it was easy for me to decide to do it," said Malta, who had sanded floors in civilian life. "It had to be done."

It was a pleasure doing it. . . . I'd do it all over again.

Malta soon found himself in Nuremberg and face to face with Hermann Goering, the Allies' prize catch.

"He was still the boss then," Malta said. "He told us we wasted too much time. I told him we had to do things by the book. He said, 'When the time comes to get me, I'll be dead.'"

Goering kept his promise, cheating Malta's noose by taking poison two hours before he was to have been executed.

As for the others, they were escorted one by one before dawn to two portable scaffolds Malta had designed so that the trap doors wouldn't swing back and strike the condemned in the head. Stacked nearby were 11 empty wooden coffins, one for Goering and one each for the 10 other condemned men.

A dozen somber journalists and generals from the major Allied powers—the United States, the Soviet Union, Britain and France—looked on as black cloth hoods were placed over the prisoners' heads. A German priest recited a short prayer. Malta pulled the lever when he reached "Amen," then went beneath the scaffold with a U.S. Army doctor to cut down the corpse.

Beside Kaltenbrunner, Frank, Sauckel and Seyss-Inquart, Malta executed Hitler's foreign minister, Joachim von Ribbentrop; chief military adviser, Field Marshal General Wilhelm Keitel; interior minister, Wilhelm Frick;

General Alfred Jodl; and anti-Jewish propagandists Alfred Rosenberg and Julius Streicher.

The hangings took just one hour and 15 minutes.

Malta left the Army in 1947 and returned to his civilian job. He keeps a tiny replica of the Landsberg Prison scaffold in the apartment he shares with his wife in this community near Boston.

Key Figures Related to the Nuremberg Trial

Sidney Alderman Member of the American prosecution team who had been the General Solicitor to the Southern Railway Company.

Murray Bernays Lawyer given the initial task of collecting evidence on crimes committed against American servicemen.

Francis Biddle U.S. Attorney General and American judge at Nuremberg.

Winston Churchill Prime Minister of Great Britain.

William Donovan Member of the American prosecution team, head of the OSS during the war.

André Gros Representative of France in war crimes commission.

Robert Jackson Legal scholar who was appointed to the Supreme Court by President Roosevelt in 1941. He took a leave of absence to serve as chief prosecutor at the Nuremberg trial.

Geoffrey Lord Lawrence Chief Justice at Nuremberg and former Lord Chief Justice of England.

David Maxwell-Fyfe Attorney General in Great Britain and head of the British prosecution team.

Henry Morganthau Jr. U.S. Secretary of the Treasury.

I.T. Nikitchenko Head of the Soviet delegation to negotiations on war crimes trials and Soviet judge during tribunal.

Franklin Delano Roosevelt President of the United States through most of World War II. Died April 12, 1945, and was succeeded by Vice President Harry Truman.

Samuel Rosenman Personal adviser to President Roosevelt.

Joseph Stalin Premier of the Soviet Union.

Henry Stimson U.S. Secretary of War.

Telford Taylor Member of the American prosecution team.

Harry Truman Vice President of the United States under Franklin Roosevelt, became president after FDR's death.

Glossary

Einsatzgruppen The four (A, B, C, D) mobile units of the Security Police and SS Security Service that followed the German armies into the Soviet Union in June 1941. Their charge was to kill all Jews as well as Soviet commissars and "mental defectives." They were supported by units of the uniformed German Order Police and used local Ukrainian, Latvian, Lithuanian, and Estonian volunteers for the killings. The victims were shot and buried in mass graves. At least 1.3 million Jews were killed in this manner.

Gestapo (*Geheime Staatspolizei*) The Nazi Secret State Police. The name was created from the first letters of the German name **Ge**heime **Sta**ats **Po**lizei. Established in Prussia in 1933, its power spread throughout Germany after 1936. The Gestapo's chief purpose was the persecution of Jews and dissident political parties. Under Himmler's direction, the Gestapo was a prime force in the murder of the six million Jews who died in the Holocaust.

NSDAP (German National Sozialistische Deutsche Arbeiter Partei) The National Socialist German Workers Party, the party led by Adolf Hitler.

OSS Office of Strategic Services. Forerunner of the Central Intelligence Agency created during World War II to carry out U.S. intelligence operations.

SA (abb. *Sturm Abteilungen*) The storm troopers, or "brown shirts," of the early Nazi party, organized in 1922.

SD (abb. *Sicherheitsdienst*) Security service of the S.S. formed in 1932 as the sole intelligence organization of the Nazi party.

SS (abb. *Schutzstaffel*) Nazi apparatus established in 1925, which later became the "elite" organization of the Nazi party and carried out central tasks in the "Final Solution." Headed by Heinrich Himmler, it became the most powerful organization of the Nazi party, virtually a state within a state.

Sipo   (Ger. *Sicherheitspolizei*) The Security Police composed of the Gestapo and the Kripo.

Wehrmacht   German armed forces.

Chronology

February 1945
President Franklin Roosevelt, Prime Minister Winston Churchill, and Premier Joseph Stalin meet in Yalta and agree to prosecute Axis leaders for war crimes at the conclusion of World War II.

April 30, 1945
Adolf Hitler commits suicide in his Berlin bunker.

May 2, 1945
President Harry Truman appoints associate supreme court justice Robert Jackson as chief U.S. counsel for the prosecution of Nazi war criminals.

May 6, 1945
Reichsmarschall Hermann Goering surrenders to the Allies.

May 7, 1945
General Alfred Jodl agrees to Germany's unconditional surrender ending World War II in Europe.

May 23, 1945
British troops capture Flensburg, Germany, and capture several top Nazi officials who later will be tried at Nuremberg. Hitler's top leader, Heinrich Himmler, commits suicide.

June 26, 1945
Robert Jackson and his counterparts from Britain, France, and the Soviet Union meet in London to decide how to proceed with the prosecution of the Germans responsible for the war.

July 7, 1945
While the Soviets advocate holding the war crimes trial in the area they control in Berlin, Robert Jackson proposes the city of Nuremberg. While almost the entire city was destroyed during the war, the Palace of Justice survived and is ultimately accepted as the site for the trial.

August 8, 1945
The Allies reach a final agreement on the prosecution of war criminals, known as the London Agreement for the location in which it is signed.

September 5, 1945
Truman decides to name former attorney general Francis Biddle as the American judge at Nuremberg.

October 14, 1945
British representative Sir Geoffrey Lawrence is elected president of the International Military Tribunal.

October 19, 1945
Indictments are issued against the major war figures.

October 25, 1945
One of the prisoners awaiting trial, Robert Ley, former chief of the German Labor Front, commits suicide.

November 20, 1945
The trial of the major war criminals by the International Military Tribunal begins at 10 a.m. in Nuremberg, Germany.

November 21, 1945
The defendants plead "Not Guilty" and the trial begins with Robert Jackson's opening statement for the prosecution.

November 29, 1945
The prosecution shows a film of Nazi atrocities in the courtroom that provides graphic images to supplement the often dry documentary and oral evidence.

December 13, 1945
The prosecution introduces particularly gruesome examples of concentration camp atrocities, including human skin with unusual tattoos that were used by the Buchenwald commandant's wife in lamp shades and the head of an executed Pole used as a paperweight by Commandant Karl Koch.

December 18, 1945
The prosecution begins its case against the seven German organizations: the Nazi party leadership, the German High Command, the SS, the SA, the SD, the Reich Cabinet, and the Gestapo.

January 8, 1946
The prosecution begins its case against the individual defendants.

March 6, 1946
The prosecution rests its case.

March 8, 1946
The defense begins its case.

July 30, 1946
The defense of the seven indicted Nazi organizations begins.

August 30, 1946
Testimony is completed in the Major War Criminals Trial.

August 31, 1946
The defendants are permitted to make statements.

September 2, 1946
The justices retire to deliberate.

October 1, 1946
The verdicts are announced, and eleven of the twenty-one defendants are sentenced to death.

October 13, 1946
The appeals of the convicted Nazis are rejected.

October 15, 1946
Goering commits suicide by swallowing a smuggled cyanide pill.

October 16, 1946
The ten surviving defendants sentenced to death are hanged in Nuremberg.

For Further Research

Zvi Aharoni et al., *Operation Eichmann: The Truth About the Pursuit, Capture, and Trial.* New York: John Wiley and Sons, 1997.

Hannah Arendt, *Eichmann in Jerusalem: A Report on the Banality of Evil.* New York: Penguin, 1994.

Mitchell G. Bard, *The Complete Idiot's Guide to World War II.* New York: Macmillan, 1998.

———, *Forgotten Victims: The Abandonment of Americans in Hitler's Camps.* Boulder, CO: Westview Press, 1994.

Michael Berenbaum, *The World Must Know: The History of the Holocaust as Told in the United States Holocaust Memorial Museum.* Boston: Little, Brown, 1993.

Joseph Borkin, *The Crime and Punishment of I.G. Farben.* New York: Free Press, 1978.

William J. Bosch, *Judgment on Nuremberg.* Chapel Hill: University of North Carolina Press, 1970.

Central Commission for Investigation of German Crimes in Poland, *German Crimes In Poland.* New York: Howard Fertig, 1982.

Richard Chesnoff, *Pack of Thieves: How Hitler and Europe Plundered the Jews and Committed the Greatest Theft in History.* New York: Doubleday, 1999.

Robert E. Conot, *Justice at Nuremberg.* New York: Carroll and Graf, 1984.

Belinda Cooper, *War Crimes: The Legacy of Nuremberg.* New York: TV Books, 1999.

Jack Fishman, *Long Knives and Short Memories.* New York: Richardson and Steirman, 1987.

Israel Gutman, ed., *Encyclopedia of the Holocaust.* Vols. 1–4. New York: Macmillan, 1995.

Gideon Hausner, *Justice in Jerusalem.* New York: Schocken, 1978.

Joe Heydecker, *The Nuremberg Trial: A History of Nazi Germany as Revealed Through the Testimony at Nuremberg.* Westport, CT: Greenwood Press, 1975.

Robert Jackson, *The Nuremberg Case*. New York: Knopf, 1947.

Robert J. Lifton, *The Nazi Doctors: Medical Killings and the Psychology of Genocide*. New York: BasicBooks, 1986.

Michael R. Marrus, *The Nuremberg War Crimes Trial of 1945–46: A Documentary History*. Boston: Bedford Books, 1997.

Werner Maser, *Nuremberg: A Nation on Trial*. New York: Scribner, 1979.

Nazi Conspiracy and Aggression. Vol. IV. Washington, DC: Government Printing Office, 1946.

Airey Neave, *On Trial at Nuremberg*. Boston: Little, Brown, 1979.

Moshe Pearlman, *The Capture and Trial of Adolf Eichmann*. New York: Simon and Schuster, 1963.

Joseph Persico, *Nuremberg: Infamy on Trial*. New York: Viking, 1994.

Drexel Sprecher, *Inside the Nuremberg Trial: A Prosecutor's Comprehensive Account*. Lanham, MD: University Press of America, 1999.

Bruce M. Stave and Michele Palmer, *Witnesses to Nuremberg*. New York: Twayne, 1998.

Telford Taylor, *The Anatomy of the Nuremberg Trials*. New York: Little, Brown, 1993.

Trial of the Major War Criminals Before the International Military Tribunal. Nuremberg: IMT, 1947.

Trials of War Criminals. Washington, DC: Government Printing Office, 1950.

Ann Tusa and John Tusa, *The Nuremberg Trial*. New York: McGraw-Hill, 1985.

Jochen von Lang, ed., *Eichmann Interrogated: Transcripts from the Archives of the Israeli Police*. New York: Farrar, Straus and Giroux, 1983.

Charles Whiting, *The Hunt for Martin Bormann: The Truth*. New York: Combined Books, 1996.

———, *Massacre at Malmédy*. New York: Combined Books, 1996.

Index

About the Editor

Mitchell Bard is the executive director of the nonprofit American-Israeli Cooperative Enterprise (AICE) and a foreign policy analyst who lectures frequently on U.S.-Middle East policy. Dr. Bard is also the webmaster for the Jewish Virtual Library (www.JewishVirtualLibrary.org), the world's most comprehensive online encyclopedia of Jewish history and culture.

Bard holds a Ph.D. in political science from UCLA and a master's degree in public policy from Berkeley. He received his B.A. in economics from the University of California, Santa Barbara. He lives in Maryland with his wife, Marcela, and sons, Ariel and Daniel.